4-6gr

W9-AXB-936

J
92
Do

9823

Myers, Elizabeth P.
Frederick Douglas; boy
champion of human rights

Frederick Douglass

Boy Champion of Human Rights

Illustrated by Robert Doremus

Frederick Douglass

Boy Champion of Human Rights

By Elisabeth P. Myers

THE **BOBBS-MERRILL** COMPANY, INC.
A SUBSIDIARY OF HOWARD W. SAMS & CO., INC.
Publishers • INDIANAPOLIS • NEW YORK

LIBRARY OF CONGRESS CATALOG CARD NUMBER: 78-127587

PRINTED IN THE UNITED STATES OF AMERICA

For my grandson, Phillip

Illustrations

Contents

Books by Elisabeth P. Myers

EDWARD BOK: YOUNG EDITOR
FREDERICK DOUGLASS: BOY CHAMPION OF HUMAN RIGHTS
F. W. WOOLWORTH: FIVE AND TEN BOY
GEORGE PULLMAN: YOUNG SLEEPING CAR BUILDER
KATHERINE LEE BATES: GIRL POET

★ Frederick Douglass

Boy Champion of Human Rights

Life with Aunt Betsey

FIVE-YEAR-OLD Fred Bailey squatted on the hard-packed dirt outside the cabin. He held a kernel of corn between his brown fingers. "Come squirrel, squirrel!" he said softly, making a soft chirruping sound in his throat.

A red squirrel, running along the rail fence, stopped and flirted its tail. Fred chirruped again, and the squirrel jumped to the ground. Then Fred held himself as still as a stone, and the squirrel inched itself closer to him step by careful step.

A slight noise from the cabin broke the spell. The squirrel scampered away even before Fred's grandmother, Aunt Betsey Bailey, appeared in the doorway with a large wooden bucket.

"Here, Fred," she said. "Will you take this bucket and get me some water from the well?"

Fred popped the kernel of corn into his mouth and ran to his grandmother. "Yes, I'll get some water," he said proudly, taking the bucket from his grandmother's outstretched hands.

The old brick well was close beside the cabin. Hanging over the well was a bucket fastened to one end of a long bar. The bar, in turn, was anchored between the limbs of nearby trees. When the opposite end of the bar was raised, the bucket could be lowered in the well. When the bar was pulled down, the bucket could be pulled up filled with water. Already Fred knew how to operate the bar.

He brought the bucket up brimming full of water. He unhooked the bucket carefully, trying not to spill any of the water. As he trudged slowly toward the cabin a little water sloshed over his dusty hands.

"That's fine, Fred," his grandmother called encouragingly.

She spoke a moment too soon. Suddenly Fred stumbled over a tree root in his path. He kept a tight hold on the bucket, but most of the water spilled on the ground.

Aunt Betsey made a clicking sound with her tongue. "You're lucky Old Master wasn't around to see you, Fred," she said, "or you'd get a licking for sure."

Fred shivered. He had never seen the person Aunt Betsey referred to, but he knew he and his grandmother both belonged to a man named Captain Anthony. They were the man's slaves, and he could do whatever he wanted to do with them. He could even take Fred away from his grandmother and doubtless would someday.

"When you're big enough, you'll have to go to

13

the home place," Aunt Betsey told all the children in her care.

This home place was a large Maryland plantation situated on the river Wye. It was the largest of many farms owned by Colonel Edward Lloyd. Fred's master, Captain Anthony, was chief clerk for Colonel Lloyd, though he owned several farms in Talbot County himself.

Aunt Betsey had worked faithfully for Captain Anthony for many years. When she grew too old to do field work, he had moved her to a cabin on one of his most distant farms. There he had put her in charge of all the babies born to his slave women. More often than not, these babies were the children of her own daughters, but he didn't know about this relationship. If he had known, he would have made other plans for them. His reason for separating children from their mothers was to break family ties.

Fred, having been placed in his grandmother's

care, was luckier than many other slave children. Aunt Betsey gave him the loving care of an affectionate mother, and he loved her in return. He respected and admired her, too, because she was held in high esteem by all the other Negroes in the neighborhood. Also, she had a reputation for being a very good fisherman with unusual fishing luck. The shad and herring just seemed to jump into her nets!

"Aunt Betsey was born to good luck," all of her neighbors said.

Somehow, as Fred felt the water turn the dirt under his feet into mud and squish up between his bare toes, he thought of Aunt Betsey's good luck. "I guess I was born to have bad luck," he said. Then he sniffled and wiped his nose on the sleeve of his tow-linen shirt.

Aunt Betsey put her hands on her hips. "No such thing," she said firmly. "If I remember correctly, you were born on Valentine Day,

1817. Mistress Anthony was showing a card covered with lace and red hearts which she called a Valentine. When she heard about you being born, she gave the card to me. 'Take this to the baby's mother and tell her I wish them both good luck,' she said. Your mother probably has that Valentine to this very day."

The idea was interesting to Fred, though he didn't remember ever seeing his mother. She came occasionally to visit Aunt Betsey, but always after Fred was fast asleep. This was the only time she could come because she was hired out as a field hand to a Mr. Stewart, who lived many miles away. Unless she could somehow borrow a mule to ride, she couldn't cover the distance back and forth in time to be present for roll-call at dawn.

"I think you're luckier than she is, Grandmother," Fred said as he turned back toward the well with the bucket.

This time he transferred the full bucket safely to his grandmother's hands. He followed her into the cabin and watched as she poured the water into a large black pot. She hung the pot from an iron hook dangling from a crane and swung it into the fireplace, where a small fire was burning.

"While the water's coming to a boil, we'll go down to the river to catch us a mess of herring," Aunt Betsey said.

"Both of us?" cried Fred. His grandmother seldom invited him to go fishing, so he wanted to be sure he heard her correctly.

"You're the only person I see around," Aunt Betsey answered.

Fred clapped his hands. "I'll go to get the new net!" he cried.

He knew that his grandmother had finished a new fish net just the night before. He had watched her deft fingers tie off the last knot in the pattern of string she had been weaving. He could see the new net now hanging from a post of her pine bedstead. It looked to him just like the oriole's nest that swung in a willow tree near the river.

"I was thinking of selling this new net," his grandmother objected.

Selling nets which she made was almost the only way she had of making money. She had a reputation for making nets strong and tight, and they were in demand not only in her home village of Tuckahoe but in the neighboring villages of Denton and Hillsboro.

"Do you have to sell the net?" asked Fred. What he meant was, did Aunt Betsey need the money from the sale of one net now or could she wait until allowance day.

The two days at the end of each month were set aside as the time for the slaves from the different farms to get their monthly allowance

18

of salt, corn, and pickled pork at the "home place." The amount given was never generous, and especially not to a slave like Aunt Betsey, who did not work in the fields. The allotment for the children in her care was even less.

Fortunately, Aunt Betsey not only fished but had a little patch of sweet potatoes, so she always had food for hungry stomachs. The few pennies she made from selling her fishnets went for molasses or some other kind of sweetening. She always bought the molasses at the end of the month, when she had an excuse to pass through the village.

"I'll see," Aunt Betsey said in answer to Fred's question.

She couldn't read, but she could count and she kept a calendar of sorts. Her calendar was only a square of clay beside the fireplace, where she scratched a little line every day with a sharp stick. At the beginning of each month she rubbed out the lines and started fresh on the new month.

The fire was not very bright, but except for the open door it provided the only light in the windowless log cabin. Aunt Betsey had to kneel with her face very close to the hearth in order to see her scratches. When she looked at them she found that the month was only half over. This meant she would have time to make other nets to sell.

"You can get the new net," she told Fred.

Standing on tiptoe, Fred lifted the net carefully from the bedpost. He hugged it tightly against his body, afraid he might catch it on something and tear it.

"I declare, a person would think you are carrying a baby," his grandmother said. She peered into the kettle to see whether the water was bubbling. Then she said, "Come on. Let's hurry down to the river."

They walked down the hill on which the cabin stood. In the valley below, beside the river, they came to a water mill, where the villagers brought their corn to be ground into meal. One of Fred's favorite pastimes was watching the huge millwheel turn slowly round and round. Watching the wheel was also a favorite pastime of the other children in Aunt Betsey's household. Two of them were watching it now as Fred and his grandmother came by. Two others were trying to fish in the millpond with string and hooks made of bent wire.

"Where are you going?" the children cried with one voice.

"We're going fishing," said Fred, who knew from experience that the children couldn't catch anything with their baitless hooks.

"May we go, too?" asked the others, but Aunt Betsey shook her head.

"So many of you together would scare the

fish away," she said. "You may go sometime later. Just wait awhile."

Fred took his grandmother's hand and squeezed it. She squeezed back, then freed herself. "Come," she said. "We're wasting time."

She walked on downstream, until suddenly she changed her course and waded into the water up to her waist. Fred started to follow her,

but the current pulled at his legs and he felt frightened. "It's too strong for me," he said. He started to cry, because he had wanted to hold one end of the new net.

"There's nothing to cry about," Aunt Betsey said, coming to take the net. "The rains have flooded the river, that's all. I'm having a little trouble myself."

Fred went back to the bank and sat down. He soon saw that his grandmother truly was finding it hard to keep her balance. He began to cheer up. After a few minutes, he started to pick the daisies that grew within arm's reach. When he had a lap full of them, he plaited their stems together to make a crown.

He was still working on the crown when Aunt Betsey came ashore, her net half full of small, wriggly fish. "We have enough for supper and some to salt down," she said.

Fred got up, careless of the daisies that scattered around him. He looked gloatingly at his grandmother's catch. "That's surely a fine mess!" he said, licking his lips as if already tasting the fish stew he would have for supper. He was hungry, even though he'd had a cold sweet potato to eat at midday.

The thought of the stew lent wings to Fred's feet. He raced on ahead of his grandmother, only to stop short at the top of the hill. There in front of the cabin he saw a horse-drawn wagon with a white man sitting on the seat.

Fred rushed back to tell his grandmother. "We have company, Grandmother," he cried. "There's a white man waiting in a wagon. What do you suppose he wants?"

Aunt Betsey put her free hand up to her eyes as if to shade them. "I don't have to suppose, Fred," she said, and her voice sounded as if it were cracking. "I'm afraid I know."

She quickened her steps. Fred ran to keep up

with her and tugged at her skirt. "What's the trouble, Grandmother?" he asked anxiously. "What is it?"

Aunt Betsey freed herself gently. "You'll find out soon enough," she said. "Now run away and play until I call you." As Fred stopped in the pathway, bewildered, she walked on toward the cabin and the man waiting for her in the wagon.

New Faces and New Places

FRED HURRIED BACK down to the water mill to tell the other children about their grandmother's visitor. They all wanted to see the stranger for themselves, but they knew Aunt Betsey would be cross if they came near. So they lay down flat near the top of the hill, where they could peer over the edge.

For a while there was nothing to see but the horse and wagon. The man had gone into the cabin to talk with Aunt Betsey. "I hope she doesn't forget about our fish stew," Fred said.

"I hope the stranger is not eating it," said one of his cousins.

This dreadful thought made all the children gasp. Fortunately, just then the man appeared and climbed into the wagon. He drove quickly away without sparing a nod for Aunt Betsey, who stood in the doorway.

Aunt Betsey stared at the cloud of dust he left in his wake, not moving until the sound of the wheels died quite away. Then, making a megaphone with her hands around her mouth, she called, "Children! You may come now!"

The fish stew was good and hot, and she gave them bits of corn bread to eat with it. All the while she never mentioned the visitor, and somehow Fred and his cousins knew that she didn't intend to, at least not then.

Days passed, and the memory of the visitor dimmed. Fred would have forgotten him entirely, except that since his visit, Grandmother seemed different. Somehow she was quieter. She didn't sing quite so often. Occasionally, when Fred was lying in the loft, half awake, half asleep, he heard her make moaning sounds. Could she be sick, he wondered?

One summer morning, a few weeks later, Aunt Betsey roused all the children early. "Fred and I are going for a long walk," she said. "Mr. Lee, at the mill, is going to keep an eye on the rest of you. Do what he tells you to do."

She gave Fred the linen shirt which she had washed and ironed for him after he had gone to bed the night before. She wound a crisp white bandanna turban around her head. She picked up bits of fish and corn bread which she had wrapped in a clean rag. Then she sent all the children outside, stepped out herself, and closed the cabin door firmly behind her.

Fred felt all tingly. He and Grandmother must be going a long way, because she almost never closed that door in the summer time. Where could they be going?

28

Aunt Betsey didn't explain anything to him. She just set out down the road, without even looking back to see whether he was following her. He had to run to stay near her. Soon his legs became tired and he began to lag farther and farther behind. Finally she turned back and picked him up. Being carried made him feel ashamed, and he said, "I'm not a baby, Grandmother! Put me down, please!"

Grandmother put him back down. "Try to keep up then," she said. "We're still a long way from where we're going."

The road grew less and less open and finally ran into a forest. At first, Fred was glad to be where it was dark and cool. The glare of the sun on the unshaded road had made him very hot. Before long, however, he began to think the dark forest was full of bad things. Tree limbs clutched at his clothes, and logs and stumps looked like fierce animals. His heart began to pound. He pressed close to his grandmother and wound his fingers in a fold of her skirt.

In a clearing, where there was a brook, Aunt Betsey stopped. "We'll have something to eat and sit for a while," she said. "Put your feet in the water to rest them."

Fred was barefoot, as usual, because he had no shoes. Besides, he had no stockings, jacket, or pants, nor was he likely to have any for years. The only clothing a slave child had until he was old enough to work in the field was a long shirt, which hung to his knees. Two shirts a year each was the allowance for both boys and girls, winter and summer.

Aunt Betsey's sitting spell lasted only a few minutes. Then she was up and trudging on, and Fred had no choice but to follow.

They left the woods behind and came to huge fields of wheat, rye, oats, corn, and tobacco which stretched out in every direction. Many men and women were working in the fields, their arms and bodies bending and twisting. They seemed to be keeping time to the songs which they were singing, or to the rhythmic chirp of the insects that were everywhere.

Fred was interested in what he saw, because everything was different from the country around Aunt Betsey's cabin. The soil in her neighborhood was too poor for growing grain and tobacco. The people there had little means of making a living except by fishing in the river.

"All the workers seem to be having fun," Fred said to his grandmother.

Aunt Betsey snorted. "Don't be fooled by their singing, child," she said. "They have to sing while they work. Overseers are afraid that quiet slaves might be thinking, and thinking could lead to trouble."

"How, Grandmother?" Fred asked, but Aunt Betsey didn't answer.

The shadows grew longer and longer as the afternoon advanced. At last Aunt Betsey walked between two big stone posts into a deeply rutted cart road, and Fred guessed they had almost reached their destination. He was glad, because he was very, very tired.

The cart road ended in a great yard filled with both noisy children and noisy animals. The children varied in color from black, brown, and copper-colored to almost white. The animals included chickens, ducks, and other feathered creatures, dogs and cats, and even a little curly-tailed pig. Altogether they made such a racket with their clucking and quacking, their bow-wowing and their squeals, that Fred held his hands over his ears.

Aunt Betsey took one of his hands and led him up a few steps into a big room. There another Negro woman was cutting vegetables into a bowl. She stopped when she saw them coming.

"Is this the new boy, Betsey?" she said, nodding at Fred, who moved closer to Aunt Betsey.

Aunt Betsey nodded in answer. "Yes, and his name is Fred."

"Fred," the other woman said. "Well, you may call me Aunt Katy."

Fred did not answer. He only stood and looked at the floor.

"Is he stubborn?" asked Aunt Katy.

"No, he's a good boy," Aunt Betsey said. She smoothed Fred's stubbly head. "Go out now and play with the other children."

"I'd rather stay here," Fred said.

Aunt Betsey took him to the door. Then she pointed to certain children and said, "Those are your brothers and sisters. The others are cousins like the children back in Tuckahoe. Go and play with them."

She gave him a little push and he walked reluctantly down the steps. At first the children were so busy playing some kind of game with pebbles that they didn't notice him. They were having so much fun he was curious and moved closer to see what they were playing.

The children had drawn a number of squares in the hard-packed dirt and were tossing pebbles into them. Sometimes one child's pebble would hit another's pebble and knock it out of a square. Then there were shouts of glee and cries of disappointment and distress.

One of the children whom Aunt Betsey had pointed out as Fred's sister finally noticed him and smiled at him. "You're Fred and I'm Sarah," she said. "We have the same mammy."

The other children stopped playing. They crowded around Fred, giving him their names as Sarah had done. His brother's name was Perry, and another sister's name was Eliza.

"Do you want to play?" Perry asked. "Here, take my shooters. I'll get some others."

Fred was surprised but took the three pebbles which Perry handed him. They were warm from Perry's fingers, and smooth.

Perry immediately darted off to the stone driveway that led to the front of the house. He returned shortly, clutching a new supply of pebbles. "I didn't get caught," he said with evident pride to the other children.

Fred was puzzled by this remark. "Get caught by what?" he asked.

"By anybody," Perry answered, but made no further explanation.

Fred was used to getting no answers or only partial answers from grown-ups. He knew better than to repeat his question, but Perry wasn't a grown-up. "Who is anybody?" he persisted.

The children looked at one another strangely and Sarah shook her head slightly. "Oh, just one of the uncles," Perry finally said.

The answer didn't help Fred very much. In

slave talk, "Uncle" and "Aunt" didn't mean kinship. They were titles of respect.

"Let's play," said Sarah quickly. "Fred can go first." She showed Fred how to step up to the line to get ready to shoot. "Keep track of all the stones you have," she warned. "The player who has the most stones left after everybody has shot is the winner."

Fred nodded. He had already guessed that having the most stones was important. "Toe up," said the other children, crowding around.

Fred toed up to the line and tossed. His first two pebbles bounced into a square and out. "You throw too hard," Eliza said.

Thanks to her warning, Fred's last shot was successful. The stone stayed smack in the middle of the center square. He could not hold back letting out an exclamation of pleasure. "Next time I throw the pebbles I'll get all of them in!" he promised himself.

His pleasure was short-lived. The very next child to shoot knocked Fred's pebble out of the square and he didn't have a chance to throw again. By now the other children were tired of playing and suggested looking for windfalls.

Fred didn't have to be told what windfalls were. He knew that the children were referring to apples, peaches, and pears that had fallen from the trees. Usually windfalls rotted easily. A person was lucky if he got a few good bites from one, but they were about the only sorts of fruit that Fred had ever tasted.

His mouth watered at the idea of biting into a juicy peach or pear, however damaged it might be. Many hours had passed since he and his grandmother had eaten fish and bread in the forest. Even so, he made no move to follow the other children. He didn't want to go off anyplace where his grandmother couldn't find him when she was ready to leave.

Sarah came and took him by the hand. "Come on. It isn't far," she said, and pulled him so that he had to go along.

They had barely reached the orchard, it seemed, when a child who had left them earlier came running. "Fred! Fred!" he cried. "Your grandmother is gone!"

"No!" Fred cried, but the fear he felt in the pit of his stomach made him sure the child had spoken the truth. With tears streaming down his cheeks, he hurried to see for himself. When he reached the kitchen yard, he ran up the steps and into the house.

Inside the kitchen he found Aunt Katy all alone, cutting up vegetables as before. He didn't wait to ask where his grandmother was but turned and ran out again. This time he ran a little way down the cart path along which he and she had come to the house.

Aunt Betsey was nowhere in sight. Fred lay

down in the path and sobbed and sobbed. Soon Sarah and Perry and Eliza came and knelt down beside him. "Don't cry," they said, and offered him peaches and pears.

Fred wouldn't be comforted. "She didn't even say good-bye!" he wailed.

"She couldn't," Sarah said. "Old Master wouldn't have wanted her to."

"Old Master!" Fred repeated. He sat up with a jerk. "Is this the home place?"

Sarah stared at him. "Why, of course it is. You mean that you didn't know?"

Fred shook his head.

"Well, now you know," Perry said. "If you're smart, you'll stop crying. Otherwise you might get a licking the very first day you are here."

All Fred could do was shake his head again.

Asking for
Trouble

THE CLANGING of a bell brought frightened looks to the faces of Fred's brother and sisters. "Aunt Katy is waiting for us," Perry said. "If we don't hurry, we won't get any supper!"

Fred felt too sick to want anything to eat, but he knew it was useless to stay where he was. He took the outstretched hands of his two sisters and walked between them to the house, crying as he went.

Aunt Katy was waiting on the kitchen stoop. She glared at Fred and said, "It won't do any good for you to cry for your grandmother. You probably never will see her again."

Fred broke out in a fresh burst of crying. Aunt Katy reached out a skinny arm and yanked him into the house. "I won't stand for all this foolish crying," she said.

With these words she shoved Fred into a closet that opened off the kitchen. He fell to his knees on a rough dirt floor. "For that, you'll go hungry tonight," she said. The she closed the door, leaving him in darkness.

Fred lay where he had fallen. He could not help continuing to cry, but he stifled the sound against his bare arm. Gradually, his eyes grew heavy and he fell asleep.

The next morning Aunt Katy opened the door to rouse him and he sprang to his feet. "Are you ready to be sensible?" she asked.

Fred nodded and she looked at him. "Does the cat have your tongue?" she asked.

"No, ma'am," said Fred, shaking his head.

"That's better," she said. "Now you can eat,

and this once I'll give you a head start on all the other children."

She pointed to a sort of trough which was filled with a mixture of coarse cornmeal and water. Fred hesitated, because he saw no utensil, such as a spoon or cup, to eat with.

"What's the matter?" Aunt Katy asked sharply. "Are you too proud to eat your meals with your hands?"

Again Fred shook his head. "No, ma'am," he said. He cupped both hands together, scooped up some mush, and poured it into his mouth. Then he chewed, swallowed, and scooped up some mush again. He repeated the same routine until trampling footsteps outside warned of the other children's approach.

"That's enough," Aunt Katy said when she heard the sound. "Step aside now."

Fred was still hungry, but he stepped aside as Aunt Katy had ordered. He wiped his mouth on his sleeve and his hands on his shirttail. Immediately the other children rushed to find places at the feeding trough. Within a few minutes the trough was empty.

"Now go back outdoors," said Aunt Katy.

The other children left, but Fred lingered inside. He didn't know what was expected of him. Would Aunt Katy tell him? Or would Captain Anthony, the old master whom he had heard so much about, come to tell him?

The thought of actually seeing Captain Anthony made Fred shiver. Every time he had heard the slaveholder's name, the threat of a licking had been mentioned. Would it be possible to please him and avoid a licking, he wondered.

"Didn't you hear me tell you to get out?" Aunt Katy said, brandishing a cooking spoon.

This time Fred didn't bother to answer. He scooted for the open door, where Sarah and Perry were waiting for him. "We'll show you around," they said, "Then if you get sent somewhere, you'll know where to go."

Fred was eager to see what this strange place was like. So far, all he had seen of the home place were a kitchen and a yard. He supposed they were part of Captain Anthony's house, and he was nearly right. As long as Captain Anthony remained Colonel Lloyd's chief clerk, the substantial brick house containing Aunt Katy's kitchen would be his.

Captain Anthony's house stood on a little hill in the center of the plantation village. Below his house were a great many other habitations. One of these, called the "Long Quarter," was a long, low, rough building housing slaves of all ages, conditions, and sizes. Another tall and rickety building served as a dormitory for hundreds of other slaves. In addition, there were dozens of little log and mud huts, similar to the cabin where Fred had lived at Tuckahoe.

"Who lives down there?" Fred asked.

"House servants, mostly," said Sarah, "or any other slaves Mr. Sevier favors."

"Who is Mr. Sevier?" Fred asked next.

"The overseer," Perry answered. "He's the man in charge of Colonel Lloyd's slaves."

Perry's choice of words puzzled Fred. "What do you mean by Colonel Lloyd's slaves?" he asked. "Aren't we his slaves, too?"

"Of course not," said Perry. "We belong to Old Master."

Still Fred didn't understand, so this time Sarah chimed in. "None of Old Master's working slaves live here," she explained. "They're on his farms, in Tuckahoe, or rented out someplace. We children aren't big enough to work, so he puts us in Aunt Katy's charge."

This information was disturbing to Fred. He had a feeling that he had started off on the wrong foot with Aunt Katy, and that life under her rule would be anything but pleasant. "Who is in charge of Aunt Katy?" he asked.

"Just Old Master," Sarah explained. "She's to him what he is to Colonel Lloyd. So with all of us children, her word is law."

They had passed the slave houses now and were in the business part of the village. All around were storehouses, tobacco houses, and barns. There also were blacksmith's shops, wheelwright's shops, and cooper's shops, more kinds of shops than Fred had ever seen before.

The roaring of the forge fire, the whirr of turning wheels, the banging of hammers interested Fred. He would have liked to stay and watch each man work, but Sarah and Perry kept urging him on. "You haven't seen the Great House yet," they cried, their voices promising something wonderful to behold.

Wonderful it was! Fred gasped at the sight of the immense three-storied white frame house, with wings on three sides. In front there was a large two-storied portico or veranda, supported by a long line of white columns that extended the entire length of the building.

"There's where we get the pebbles for our game," said Perry, pointing to the driveway leading up to the house.

Fred looked at the wide drive. It formed a circle around a beautiful green lawn and led off between overhanging shade trees toward a distant ornamental gate. The lawn was planted with blossoming shrubs and flowers, all lending sweet perfume to the air.

For a moment, Fred stared at the beautiful scene. Then he was not able to stand just looking any longer. He darted across the drive and stooped to stroke the smooth green grass. Then suddenly he came upon an older white boy standing directly in front of him. "Why are you here?" asked the boy. "What were you doing?"

"I wasn't doing anything," Fred said quickly.

"You had to be," the other boy answered, but he didn't sound cross.

"I was just feeling, I guess," Fred said. "I never saw such pretty grass before."

"You ought to lie down on it," the other boy said as he lay down to demonstrate. "Come on and try it!" he invited.

Fred hesitated, but his curiosity was so great that he lay down, too. The beautiful grass made the softest bed he had ever known, and it smelled fresh and sweet. As he lay there, he was happier than he had been any time since his grandmother had left.

"I'm Daniel Lloyd," the white boy said.

At once Fred was filled with fright. Here he was lying on the grass with the son of the plantation owner! He had been invited, but he shouldn't be there and he had better not stay.

Quickly he jumped up and looked over to

where he had left Sarah and Perry. They were almost hidden behind tree trunks at the edge of the yard, as if trying to stay out of sight.

"I have to go, Master Daniel," said Fred, hurrying to rejoin his brother and sister.

The two children grasped his hands and pulled him hastily after them back toward the slave village. "You're just asking for trouble by such actions," Sarah scolded. "We're not allowed to play around the Big House!"

"Master Daniel invited me to lie on the grass," Fred said.

"He'll likely be sorry, too, if anybody saw you," Perry said.

Fred didn't know what to say in return. He couldn't seem to do anything right here at the home place. Yet here he was.

They now were in the main village. Fred's attention was distracted by a rhythmic tap! tap! tap! nearby. He looked around, expecting to see a woodpecker drumming on a hollow log. "Uncle Abel's making shoes," Perry explained. "Let's go watch him for a minute."

They went into a small shed, where a round-shouldered little man sat astride a saddle-shaped bench. He was hammering nails into a piece of leather propped up on a foot-sized stand before him. When he saw the children, he paused. "This is Fred Bailey, Uncle Abel," Sarah said.

Uncle Abel mumbled something through his mouthful of tacks. Then, realizing that he couldn't speak clearly, he spit the tacks into his hand. "Are you another of Harriet's children?" he asked asked loudly and clearly.

"I guess so," replied Fred, for he knew his mother's name was Harriet.

"May we watch?" Perry asked.

Uncle Abel nodded. "I'm getting some shoes ready for next allowance day," he said.

He kept a few tacks loose in his hand. Then,

52

popping the others back into his mouth, he returned to his job.

Fred was fascinated by the routine, as Uncle Abel smoothed the leather, inserted a tack, hammered. His actions were as rhythmic as music, Fred thought. Smooth, insert, and hammer! Smooth, insert, and hammer!

Fred would have liked to watch the shoemaker for a long time, but the other children grew restless. "I'm hungry," Perry said. "Maybe Aunt Katy will give us some bread if we go to the kitchen and ask her politely."

The mere thought of bread made Fred's mouth water. He hadn't had anything to eat except a few scoops of mush since he had eaten lunch with his grandmother the noon before. He was hungry, but he wasn't hopeful about getting any bread. His experience with Aunt Katy hadn't given him any reason to hope.

Aunt Katy was beating a carpet spread out

on the grass. When she saw Fred, she raised the broom and hit at him. "This is your first day here and already you're acting uppity!" she yelled.

Fred ducked and put his arms over his face to protect himself. He didn't ask what he had done to deserve this kind of treatment. He guessed that somehow word of his daring to lie on the grass was causing the trouble.

"Get out of my sight and stay out!" Aunt Katy ordered. "And don't come around expecting any supper. I'll starve you into knowing your place around here, that's what I'll do!"

The only place where Fred knew to go to keep out of her sight was the little closet where she had shoved him the night before. He crept back in, lay down on the floor, and gave way to tears. This time, he cried more from fright than from loneliness. Since he had no way of knowing what his place was, he was almost certain that Aunt Katy would starve him to death.

Somebody's Child

FRED LAY IN the dark closet for a long time. Through cracks in the wall, he could peer out into the kitchen. What he saw and what he smelled almost tortured him. A whole skinned animal of some sort was turning on a spit over the fireplace. Great pots of something savory were steaming on the iron stove. At a table, Aunt Katy was mixing flour and water into a batter and rolling it flat. Then she filled the batter with sliced fruit and put it into a pan.

Fred had never seen or smelled such mouth-watering goodies before, but he knew better than to expect to get to eat any of them. Undoubtedly they were intended for Old Master's table, and not for the slaves.

At sundown Aunt Katy rang the bell to call the other children to supper. A few minutes later she called Fred from his hiding place. His hopes rose. Maybe she hadn't meant what she said! Maybe she would give him something to eat after all. His hopes were in vain.

She gave great chunks of corn bread and pieces of pork fat to the others, but gave nothing to Fred. His sisters gave him sad looks, but there was nothing they could do to help him. They could not even save him a portion of their own food. Aunt Katy kept them under watchful eye until their food was gone.

After supper, all the children were expected to get out from underfoot again. Most of them went off to their sleeping places. Fred went outdoors, thinking perhaps he could go to the orchard and find some fruit to eat.

This hope, too, was in vain. By now it was night and there was no light to guide him. He groped his way back to the kitchen steps and sat down. Tears rolled down his cheeks again, and he was so miserable he wished that he could die and be done with it.

For a time he could hear Aunt Katy moving in the kitchen, but after while everything became quiet. Cautiously he got up and peeked inside. Nobody was there!

Hope rose again. Maybe Aunt Katy had left some food out, where he could get it. He looked all around the kitchen, but all he could find was an ear of dried Indian corn on a shelf. He stood on tiptoe and managed to reach the ear. He tore off some kernels with his finger nails and put the cob good side forward on the shelf again. Then he shoved the loose corn into the still-warm ashes of the fire to roast.

By now Fred was so hungry that he snatched

out some of the kernels before they were even warm. Before he could start eating, Aunt Katy came back into the kitchen with another woman. The woman looked at Fred and gave a little cry. "My little boy!" she said, hastening to throw her arms around him.

Fred did not know who the woman was, but her kind welcome started him crying again. The woman misinterpreted his tears. "Don't be afraid of me!" she said. "I'm your mother!"

"I'm not afraid of you," he said, sobbing. "I was afraid I would starve to death!" He raised a handful of kernels to his mouth.

His mother quickly dashed the kernels to the floor. "Nobody is going to threaten to starve my son!" she said, darting such a threatening look toward Aunt Katy that the cook almost seemed to shrink in size. "Get him something good to eat at once!"

Aunt Katy was stunned and unable to move. She just stood still, her mouth opening and closing like that of a new-caught fish.

"All right, I'll get him something myself!" Fred's mother said. She went to the larder and took down a beautiful, spicy-smelling cake and gave it to Fred.

Hungry though he was, Fred stared at the delicacy in his hand. It was heart-shaped and covered on top with a dark sugary glaze. It was so pretty Fred could scarcely believe it was meant to be eaten.

His mother saw his hesitation. "Eat your gingerbread, for goodness' sake!" she said. "And when you finish, if you're still hungry, you can have some more."

At that Aunt Katy made a sharp, protesting sound, a kind of yip. Fred, afraid that she might snatch the gingerbread away, began hastily to eat. His mother sat down in a rocker by the fire. She pulled Fred onto her lap and cradled him fondly. Then, while he continued to eat, she gave Aunt Katy a tongue-lashing.

"If you ever threaten to starve my child to death again, I'll know about it," she said. "I'll learn about it the same way I learned he had been brought here. Also the next time I'll tell

60

Old Master how you are treating him and you know what that will mean!"

Fred did not know how his mother had found out about his coming there. Later he learned that she was thought to be clairvoyant, a person who knew about things that were to happen before they took place. Right now, though, he could see that Aunt Katy was frightened by his mother's words. He guessed she would treat him less harshly, at least for a while.

That thought, plus the fullness of his stomach and the warmth of his mother's embrace, made Fred relax. His mother spoke to him softly from time to time and crooned to him. She sang the same lullaby his grandmother had sung to the newest baby in her cabin family.

> "Hushabye,
> Don't you cry,
> Go to sleep, little baby;
> When you wake

You shall have
All the pretty little horses;
Blacks and bays,
Dapples and grays,
Coach and six little horses.
Hushabye,
Don't you cry,
Go to sleep, little baby."

Before his mother reached the refrain of the second verse, Fred was sound asleep. The next morning when he awoke, he was lying on the fireplace hearth. He rubbed his eyes, sat up, and looked about the room. Aunt Katy was the only person he saw. For a moment, he wondered if he had dreamed his mother had been there.

"It won't do you any good to look for your mother," Aunt Katy said. "She's gone."

Her words cheered Fred rather than saddened him. Now he knew that seeing his mother the night before had not been a dream. He no longer was just a child, he was somebody's child. Even if he never saw his mother again, he would know that she cared for him. He would never forget how thoughtful she looked or how tenderly she had smiled at him.

The influence of Fred's mother lingered with Aunt Katy, too. The old cook was often mean after that, but no more so to Fred than to the other children. Sometimes they got smaller servings of food than they wanted at mealtime, but they always got something. Still, Fred had been used to far more nourishment before he came here than he got from Aunt Katy.

At times Fred became so hungry that he resorted to lying under the kitchen table. He had noticed that Aunt Katy often threw scraps of food there for old Nep, the dog. He even risked getting bitten, in order to grab bits of meat and bread before old Nep could get them.

Except for never getting enough to eat, Fred lived contentedly during the succeeding months.

He was too young to work in the fields, and there was little other work a child his age could do. Occasionally he did a little sweeping or brought the cows from their pasture. Otherwise, he and the other youngsters ran loose over the plantation together.

There were many wonderful places to explore nearby. One of Fred's favorite spots was on Long Point, a tract of land that lay between Miles River and the River Wye. He became interested in an old wooden tower-type windmill which was used for draining the land. All the machinery was located in the tower, which was capped by a movable roof. At the top there were sails or wings, which were connected with the machinery by gears. When the wind caught the sails, they turned the machinery.

Fred found the sails fascinating. He loved to watch them turning against a background of the sky. He enjoyed listening to the clank of the machinery as it drained the land and pumped the water into the river.

Offshore in the Wye River lay another object of enchantment for Fred. It, too, had sails, but they were made of canvas instead of wood. This was a large white boat named the "Sally Lloyd" in honor of Colonel Lloyd's daughter. It was used to carry products from the plantation to market in Baltimore or Annapolis.

Occasionally, Fred went to Long Point when the time came for the "Sally Lloyd" to sail. All the crew would bustle about on deck for what seemed a very long time. At last, up would go the white mainsail and the jib. Then up would come the anchor, and off the "Sally Lloyd" would go, her sails filled with wind.

The sight of the boat sailing away pleased Fred, but it filled him with intense longing. What did it feel like to sail away like that, free as a bird? Would he ever know?

Fred Learns a
Hard Lesson

LONG POINT was only one of many places where
Fred spent his playtime. Except for the formal
area close to the Great House, where he had
trespassed his first day, he explored all parts of
the huge plantation.

Close to the formal area, but outside it, was a
place called "the park," where Fred sometimes
went alone to sit. He had learned that, if he was
patient, he often would be rewarded by seeing
rabbits, deer, and other wild animals. He
couldn't feed the animals, as he had fed the
squirrels in Tuckahoe, but these animals didn't
seem to expect him to feed them.

A few of the animals became his close friends. Among them was a female deer. She would come up behind him and put her wet nose against his neck. Occasionally she would lick him with her rough tongue. All the while he was careful not to move a muscle, because he didn't want anything to scare her away.

A pair of raccoons also became Fred's close friends. They would crawl all over him, digging their paws into the pocket of his shirt and tucking their heads into the curve of his arm. Then they would sit and look at him with beady eyes from behind their black masks.

The raccoons also allowed Fred to hold and stroke them, and he was glad to have warm, livnig things to cuddle. He had enjoyed little cuddling in his own life, only a few rockings in his grandmother's arms, and he found it pleasant and satisfying. He didn't realize yet that slaves were not supposed to have emotions—that slaveholders tried to erase their slaves' human feelings and to make them like mechanical men.

The other slave boys couldn't understand why Fred liked the park, or why he wanted to spend so much time with deer or rabbits when he could watch horses. "The stables are the place where things are going on," they said.

When Fred wanted to be where things were going on, he went to the stables, too. About thirty-five horses, all of them chosen for blood, speed, and beauty, were kept there. Their destiny in life was purely to provide pleasure for Colonel Lloyd's household. Some were trained to pull carriages in the summer and sleighs in the winter. Some were reserved for hunting with hounds. The daintiest of all were kept for gentle riding by the ladies.

Two men were in charge of the stables, a father and son, called Old Barney and Young Barney. They were one of the few family units

among Colonel Lloyd's slaves. He kept them together because of their genius as horse-handlers.

"It must be nice to have a father," Fred had
said when he first heard of their relationship. He
supposed he himself had a father, but he didn't
know who he was. Slave children seldom knew
about their fathers and seldom had last names.
Fred went by his mother's last name, which was
Bailey. She knew what her last name was, because her parents, like the Barneys, had been too
valuable to be separated.

"The Barneys don't have it very easy," Fred
was told. "You'll find out sooner or later if you
stay around the stables."

The first few times Fred went to the stables
he noticed nothing disagreeable. The harness
room smelled pleasantly of leather and of the
medicines Old Barney used for treating sick
horses. The stalls were kept clean, strewn often
with fresh straw.

The horses throughout the stable were sleek and well groomed. Young Barney was always combing the mane or brushing the tail of a horse. He made sure that each horse was well shod, with feet and legs free from blemishes.

The two Barneys lived in the stable, but Fred didn't consider that a hardship. "Even if they sleep in a stall with the horses, their beds are softer than ours are," he said to the other boys. "They sleep on that straw, whereas we sleep on bare floors. Besides, it's light and airy in the stables, a lot lighter and airier than my closet off the kitchen!"

"Just the same," the boys replied, "you've no cause to envy them. You'll see."

And one day Fred saw. In later years, he referred to the scene as "one of the most heartsaddening and humiliating" he had ever witnessed. It was a scene that he never forgot.

Fred had learned from his grandmother that a

slaveholder could force a slave to do anything and that he could do anything to a slave. A slaveholder's conscience was the only thing to keep him from killing a slave, if he wanted to. Not until he saw Colonel Lloyd beat Old Barney, however, had Fred ever believed that one man could be so cruel to another person for no apparent reason.

That forenoon Fred knelt beside Old Barney, watching him apply a poultice to a mare's lame knee. The aged Negro's hands were gentle, and the animal stood quietly under his touch. Suddenly, there was the sound of trampling hoofs in the stable yard, and in a moment Colonel Lloyd came striding into the barn.

This was the first time Fred had ever seen the plantation owner, but he recognized him at once for what he was. The Colonel was elegantly dressed in riding clothes, and he wore a stovepipe hat over his silver hair. His face was red with anger and he carried a riding whip loose in one hand as if threatening to use it.

"Get into the yard and take a look at that animal I've been riding!" the Colonel ordered Old Barney. "There's a twist in his reins and dust in his hair!"

The loud voice startled the mare, but Old Barney managed to keep the wet pad in place on her sore. "Didn't you hear me, you old rascal?" shouted the Colonel, snapping his whip.

"Yes, sir," said Old Barney.

The old slave took one of Fred's hands and placed it on the poultice to hold the poultice in place. By now the mare was used to Fred and made no objection to his taking Old Barney's place. Fred had schooled himself in handling animals, so even though he lacked experience with horses, he seemed to know what to do. He just continued to hold the wet pad in place and to speak gently to the horse.

From where he knelt, he could see through the open stable door into the yard. The ground outside was damp, for rain had fallen during the night. Nevertheless, Colonel Lloyd had forced Old Barney onto his knees and ordered him to strip off his shirt.

Fred almost cried out in protest. Even if Old Barney was guilty of neglecting a horse, which Fred doubted, he shouldn't be treated in this manner. Then, to Fred's horror, Colonel Lloyd raised his horsewhip and slapped it down on Old Barney's bare shoulders.

At that, Fred gasped. The mare looked around at him curiously, but he didn't see her. He had shut his eyes tight. He couldn't help hearing what was going on in the yard, but he was determined not to see.

After awhile, the swish of the long lash stopped. Fred waited a few seconds, opened his eyes again, and saw Colonel Lloyd walk away.

Old Barney, still shirtless, was leading the Colonel's mount toward his stall in the stable. When he reached the stall the old slave sat down heavily on a three-legged stool.

"The mare is all right now," Old Barney said.

74

"Do you think you can minister to me, Fred, if I tell you what to do?"

"I can try," said Fred.

Under the old man's directions, Fred mixed flour and mustard with hot water to prepare a smooth paste. "Now soak a piece of this rag in the soft paste and dab it over my back," Old Barney said.

Fred had avoided looking at the slave's injured back, but now he had to see it. He gritted his teeth, but applied the remedy until he was told to stop.

"The mustard smarts something fierce on my back," Old Barney said, putting on his shirt, "but it will help the cuts to heal."

Just then, Young Barney came into the stable. He knew at once what had happened and he clenched his fists. "Who did it, the Colonel or one of those cowardly sons-in-law?" he asked.

Old Barney kept his lips firmly closed, so

Young Barney asked Fred. "The Colonel did it," Fred stammered.

"What was his excuse?"

"Twisted reins and dust," Fred said.

"Dust!" snorted Young Barney. "He'd been riding, hadn't he? Of course there was dust! Oh, if only I dared, I'd show him what dust is! Why did I have to be born a slave?"

That questioning cry rang again in Fred's ears that night as he lay sleepless for a while in his drafty little closet. Why was anybody born a slave? What gave some men the right to own other men?

Fred remembered his grandmother saying, "God must have planned it that way. He made all things and He knows what's good for everybody. It isn't up to us to question Him."

Until Fred had seen Old Barney whipped, he had accepted his grandmother's explanation. Now he couldn't accept it any longer. How could it be good for Old Barney to be whipped when he hadn't done anything wrong?

"If I had my way," Fred thought, "I'd throw every whip on the plantation into the river."

A few days later Fred had an experience of his own with a whip wielded by Uncle Isaac Copper. Uncle Isaac was a Negro, often called "doctor" because he served as doctor of medicine and doctor of divinity to the slaves. He was the only physician and preacher they had.

Uncle Isaac had four remedies for all the ailments of life. These four remedies were Epsom salts and castor oil for diseases of the body and the Lord's Prayer and hickory switches for diseases of the soul.

One of Uncle Isaac's soul-doctoring jobs was to teach the Lord's Prayer to children six years of age. Therefore, on the day that Aunt Katy realized that Fred was six, she ordered him to attend prayer school. Along with him she sent other children she guessed to be the proper age for instruction.

They found Uncle Isaac seated on a tall stool in an old building. Next to him, within easy reach, was a huge pile of long hickory switches. "Kneel down," he said, picking up a switch. Hurriedly the children knelt.

"Bow your heads." They bowed.

"Now repeat every word I say after me."

He recited the first two words of the prayer which Jesus taught His disciples: "Our Father," and everybody repeated them without error. The words "Who art in Heaven," also were fairly well done. But on the third portion, Fred misunderstood the word "hallowed."

He thought the word was "hollowed" and pronounced it that way. At once the hickory stick flicked across the back of Fred's head. "I told you to say everything I say! That means saying it!" Uncle Isaac stormed.

It took some weeks for Fred to learn the Lord's Prayer by heart. During that time, he often received a switching.

From his experience with Uncle Isaac, Fred learned a sobering truth. In a slave society such as his, the whip was all-important. Slaves and slaveholders alike used it as a remedy for all forms of disobedience. Nobody ever thought to try kindness and patience as remedies instead.

A Little Bit of Kindness

Kindness and patience were the exception, not the rule, on Lloyd's plantation. Luckily for Fred, he saw both virtues displayed regularly by Old Barney at the stables. He could practice them himself with wild animals. Otherwise, he might have become hard-hearted himself.

As the months passed, Fred was forced to witness other beatings besides that of Old Barney. Each time he wanted to help the victim, but he knew that he couldn't do anything alone. "It would be like one chicken against a fox," he thought. "Now if there were lots of chickens, things would be different!"

80

And one day, there were. Fred was returning from the river where he recently had learned to dig oysters and to eat them raw. He was thinking that a lunch of corn bread would be all he would want to eat.

Suddenly Fred's pleasant thoughts were interrupted by the sound of screams and curses. One of Colonel Lloyd's female slaves, named Nelly, was being dragged toward a tree by the overseer, Mr. Sevier. Evidently he planned to tie Nelly to a tree and whip her. "I'll teach you to talk back to me," he yelled.

Nelly was not as meek as many slaves. She probably had dared to stick up for herself and possibly had denied she was guilty as charged. Right or wrong, anything she said would be considered impudence on her part. Slaves weren't permitted to defend themselves. Fred had learned this, too, from Old Barney.

Nelly certainly knew she could not escape

punishment. Unlike Old Barney, however, she wasn't going to make it easy for her accuser. She started to kick and scratch.

Suddenly three of Nelly's five children came running up. "Let our mother go!" they yelled.

To Fred's delight, two of the children, who were boys, began to pelt the overseer with stones. The third, a little girl, seized hold of his leg and started to bite him.

Fred's heart gave a great leap. Here was his chance to help! In his pocket he had half a dozen oyster shells which he had saved to use as food scoops. They'd make splendid weapons, because their edges were so sharp.

One after the other, Fred aimed the shells at the overseer's face. Some brought blood, and Fred was glad. "We can't save Nelly from getting a whipping," he exulted, "but we can make Mr. Sevier sorry he picked on her!"

Overseers perferred to whip slaves who were

easily whipped. They always wanted to give punishment, never to receive it. This was valuable information for Fred. Someday he hoped to be in a position to use the information. Already, he was being given a few chores to do.

Among the things Fred was now expected to do was perform small tasks for his master's daughter, Miss Lucretia. She had recently married and returned to live in her father's house with her husband, Thomas Auld.

Fred was happy to serve Miss Lucretia. Before her marriage, she had sometimes noticed him when she came to the kitchen to talk to Aunt Katy about household matters. She had smiled at him from time to time and patted him on the head. Once she had even given him a cooky hot from the oven. He appreciated this kindness and was not likely to forget it.

The things she asked him to do were easy. On hot days, he waved a palm-leaf fan to cool her.

On cool days, he brought her foot-warming bricks, which were kept always ready on the back of the wood stove in the kitchen for just that purpose. Sometimes he held her horse's bridle while she mounted, or gave her a "hand up" as she stepped into her carriage.

It soon became routine for Fred to play under Miss Lucretia's window, so he'd be ready when she called. One day, while he was playing there, he began to sing a tune he'd learned on allowance day. A slave on one of Colonel Lloyd's ships had taught him the song. The repetition of the word "sail" had caught his fancy, and he had memorized the song quickly.

> "Sail, O believer, sail,
>   Sail over yonder,
> Sail, O my brother, sail,
>   Sail over yonder."

Miss Lucretia heard Fred singing. She leaned out the window. "I didn't know you could sing,

Fred," she said. "Do you know any more songs like that one?"

Fred shook his head. "No, ma'am," he replied, "only more of the same one." Then he sang the second verse.

> "Come view the promised land,
>   Sail over yonder.
> O brother lend a hand,
>   Sail over yonder!"

Miss Lucretia clapped her hands. "For singing that song, you deserve a reward," she said. "Stay where you are and I'll be back in a jiffy."

Fred was pleased to wait. He didn't know what a "reward" was, but it sounded pleasant. Soon Miss Lucretia returned and handed him a thick slice of white bread spread with brown sugar. His eyes shone and his mouth began to water as he took the bread. Such treats had been rare in his life.

"Eat, child, eat," Miss Lucretia said.

Fred began to eat, but he took very small bites. He wanted to make his reward last as long as possible.

After that, Fred listened closely to the songs the slaves sang. They often sang as they worked, because the overseer didn't like silent people. "Make a noise! Make a noise!" he'd shout, and crack his whip threateningly.

The slaveholders didn't know that the songs which slaves sang often had double meanings. Neither, of course, did Fred at his young age, but he realized it before he was many years older. Every tone in a song was a testimony against slavery. Every verse was a prayer to God for release from bondage.

From this time on Miss Lucretia favored Fred and Aunt Katy resented his good luck. She was jealous because she had children of her own, whom Captain Anthony had neglected to send away. Consequently, she often slapped Fred

and accused him of all manner of things. Apparently she still remembered his mother's recent threats, however, and continued to feed him with the other children.

Aunt Katy didn't care what happened to Fred when he was out of her sight. One day, a much older boy fought him with a sharp piece of cinder fused with iron from the blacksmith's forge. He received a number of long scratches and a severe gash on his forehead. The gash began to bleed freely, and the sight of the blood frightened him. He began to cry and ran back to the kitchen, seeking help.

"Serves you right," Aunt Katy said, making no effort to stop the bleeding or his crying.

Her callousness made Fred cry even louder. Miss Lucretia heard him and came hurrying to see what was the matter. "Oh, poor child!" she said, shocked.

She led Fred into Old Master's parlor and had

him lie down on the horsehair sofa. Then she brought water and soft cloths, with which she washed and bound up his wounds. "There, now you'll soon be fine," she said, "but lie there until you feel better."

Fred felt better at once, but wasn't ready to admit it yet. He'd never been in Old Master's parlor before, and he might never be there again. Now he wanted to stay there as long as he could.

Miss Lucretia went to the side of the room and started to play a melodeon, or sort of piano. Fred listened, surprised and entranced, for a little while. He felt very peaceful and comfortable, so comfortable that he fell asleep.

Fred Takes
a Trip

WHEN FRED AWOKE, he heard voices murmuring behind him. He turned over and saw Miss Lucretia talking to Old Master. His heart began to pound. Would Captain Anthony punish him for being there? Would Miss Lucretia explain?

Fred heard his name, but he was being talked about, not being talked to. He shut his eyes, pretending he was still asleep. He might as well listen to find out what was happening.

"Somehow you think Katy can do no wrong," Fred heard Miss Lucretia say to her father, "but you are mistaken. She's a regular devil in the way she treats this poor child."

"Nonsense!" sputtered Captain Anthony. "It doesn't do to coddle little pickaninnies. Coddling spoils them for the future."

"That may be," Miss Lucretia answered, "but you didn't see what I saw today."

There was silence for a moment. Fred lay very still. He knew that Miss Lucretia and her father were still looking in his direction. "Well," Captain Anthony said, "he's your boy. If you want to send him to Thomas's brother, I won't stop you."

At these words, Fred's heart beat so hard he was afraid they could hear it, but they didn't. Soon Captain Anthony left, and Miss Lucretia called softly, "Fred, wake up."

For another few heartbeats, Fred made no response. Miss Lucretia put a hand on his shoulder and shook him gently. This time Fred opened his eyes. He would have sat up, but Miss Lucretia held him back.

"Move slowly," she said, "so you don't start the bleeding again." She helped him gradually to a sitting position, then looked him over critically. "You're dirty," she said.

Fred said nothing. He looked no different than he always did. She just never had bothered to notice before. "Well, you'll have to scrub yourself clean," she continued. "Miss Sophy wouldn't want you near Tommy, otherwise."

The names Miss Sophy and Tommy meant nothing to Fred, but if Miss Lucretia wanted him to scrub himself clean, he would gladly comply. He stood up, ready to start the hard scrubbing. Miss Lucretia laughed. "Aren't you going to ask why?" she asked.

"No, ma'am," said Fred. He had often heard that slaves were wise only to say "yes" or "no" to white people. Otherwise, they might get a whipping for being familiar.

Miss Lucretia laughed again. "I'm going to

tell you anyway. You are going to Baltimore to
live with Mr. and Mrs. Hugh Auld. Mr. Auld is
my husband's brother. He wants a trustworthy
boy to look after his son Tommy."

Fred forgot his lesson about not talking.
"Baltimore!" he cried. "I'm going?"

"Yes, you," Miss Lucretia replied. "You're going Saturday." She looked at him closely again.
"You'll have to have some other clothes," she
added. "You'll need a clean shirt, and, for goodness' sake, a pair of trousers."

The thought of owning trousers was almost
as exciting to Fred as going to Baltimore. Slaves
weren't issued trousers until they became field
hands or house servants. If he was going to look
after a boy named Tommy, he probably would
be a house servant. What luck!

As soon as Miss Lucretia let him go, Fred
made a beeline for the creek. He and the other
children had often waded in the creek but had

never bathed in it. They were too afraid of getting a licking from Aunt Katy for getting their clothes wet. This time, however, Fred sat down boldly. He grabbed a handful of sand and began to scour himself.

Fred spent much of the next two days in the creek, scrubbing himself almost raw. On Friday evening, he felt that he was ready for inspection. He took his usual place under Miss Lucretia's window and began to sing.

> "I built my house upon the rock,
>   O yes, Lord!"

Miss Lucretia had evidently been expecting him, for she came out at once. "Let me look at you," she said.

She gave special attention to Fred's knees and feet, which had been particularly encrusted with dirt. Fred waited anxiously for her decision. Would he pass her careful inspection?

Apparently he would, because Miss Lucretia smiled and patted him on the head. "Stay here just a minute," she said, "while I go to get your new clothes."

The new clothing included a shirt such as Fred had been wearing for years, linen trousers, and a pair of coarse shoes. The last two items brought joy to Fred's heart, because he had never possessed either before. "Oh, thank you!" he cried, clutching them to his breast.

Pity, or some similar emotion, brought tears to Miss Lucretia's eyes. She smoothed the mound of clothes and said, "Remember to wash once you get to Baltimore, Fred. I don't want Mr. Hugh Auld to be sorry we sent you."

Fred didn't sleep much that night. He was to go by ship, which would sail at sunup the next morning, and he was afraid he'd be left behind. He didn't mind his sleeplessness, however, because he had so much to think about.

Fred had no regrets about leaving the home place. It had never been home to him, the way his grandmother's cabin in Tuckahoe had been. Except for Miss Lucretia, nobody here cared anything for him. His brothers and sisters would soon be sent away, and he had been told recently that his mother had died.

He felt that Baltimore at least would be different. He had heard about the city from the Negro boatman who had taught him the "Sail Over Yonder" song. One boatman, who was a cousin of his, had said that nothing Fred had ever seen could compare with Baltimore.

"Why, there are ships there that could carry four such sloops as Colonel Lloyd owns," he had boasted. "And some houses there would make Lloyd's Great House look very small."

That same cousin had seen a steamboat moving along and soldiers marching. He had heard bells ringing like crazy and the screams of millions of seabirds. "It's a grand place!" he told Fred. "I hope you get to see it someday!"

Now Fred was not only going to see it, he was going to live there. Even if he had to endure whippings in his new home, they could be no worse than whippings he would have had to endure on Lloyd's plantation.

Fred went aboard the sloop before dawn. One of the deck hands called Rich guided him to a place by the rail. "Stay here until it's light enough to see what you're doing," he said. "After that, just keep out of the way!"

Fred clutched the railing with trembling hands. How exciting it was to be on a boat such as he had often watched from the shore! Soon he'd be sailing down the river out into the bay. And he'd be free as a bird, at least until he reached Baltimore.

As soon as it was light, Fred walked to the stern of the sloop. He took what he hoped was his last look at Lloyd's plantation. Then, careful not to get in the path of the bustling deckhands, he went to the bow. Here he could look ahead to see where the sloop was going.

Fred spent most of the day watching what was in the distance, rather than near by. The broad bay seemed to be alive with ships of all kinds. Some had colored sails and others white sails. Fred liked white sails best, like those on his own vessel, because they looked like clouds against the blue sky.

Late in the afternoon, the sloop docked briefly at Annapolis, the capital of the state of Maryland. Fred gazed in wonder, because it was the first large town he had ever seen. He wondered whether Baltimore would be as large and grand as Annapolis.

Rich, the deckhand who seemed to have charge of him, came to lean over the railing and look with him. "This is a big place," he said.

"Yes. Is Baltimore as large and grand as this?" asked Fred.

"Well, it's larger, maybe fifty times larger," said Rich, "but I don't know about it being any grander than Annapolis."

Fred gasped. He couldn't even imagine a place that big. "What keeps a person from getting lost there, possibly on purpose?" he asked.

"By person, do you mean a slave?" Rich asked. "If you mean a slave, you would find it very hard to get lost."

"Why?" asked Fred.

"Because of the Fugitive Slave Law, that's why," replied Rich.

Fred had never heard of the Fugitive Slave Law. "What's that law?" he asked.

"I don't know what it says, but it's a law that gives slave owners the right to hunt down runaway slaves, just like foxes. Have you ever seen a fox brought back by hounds?"

Fred shuddered. He had seen this sorry sight once or twice, and hoped he'd never see it again. Just then a whistle turned their minds from the sickening subject of foxes and hounds. It was time for Rich to get to work. The ship was going to get under way again.

"Wait for me here when we get to Baltimore," Rich said. "Then I'll help you find the place where you are supposed to go."

He started to leave, but Fred pulled at his shirttail. "When do we reach Baltimore?"

"Some time tomorrow morning," Rich said.

Darkness was beginning to fall as the sloop moved away from the dock. Lights appeared in the town a few at a time, reminding Fred of the fireflies he'd chased when he was smaller.

When night had completely fallen, Fred suddenly realized he was hungry. He hadn't eaten since morning, when he'd had his usual meager meal of mush. When he had left, Aunt Katy had handed him something wrapped in corn husks. "Miss Lucretia told me to give you this," she said. "Hang onto it, because it's possibly the only supper you'll get."

Fred had wedged the package into a little space he had found under the railing. "Hallelujah!" he exclaimed when he unwrapped the package and saw two thick slices of corn bread with a chunk of salt pork between them. This generous meal, he knew, was due to Miss Lucretia's insistence, not Aunt Katy's generosity.

After he had eaten, he lay down on the deck. "Now if only Miss Sophie could be as nice to little slave boys as Miss Lucretia——" he murmured drowsily.

A Child Like Any Other

THE SLOOP tied up at Smith's wharf in Baltimore early Sunday morning. Bells seemed to be ringing everywhere, their different tones filtering through various other sounds at the dockside, including the bleating of sheep. Many sheep were being herded down a ramp to shore.

"I have to help drive the sheep to the slaughterhouse," said Rich, suddenly appearing at Fred's side. "Come along and we'll go from there to Auld's place."

Fred had helped to herd cows from the pasture to the barn on the plantation, but he'd never handled sheep before. He had only a confusing impression of the surroundings through which he walked, because he was busy watching the sheep. After they were safely penned, however, and he started off with Rich for Alliciana Street, he was too excited to see clearly.

"What are Mr. and Mrs. Hugh Auld like?" he asked, for he knew that Rich had frequently been sent on errands to the Auld home.

Rich shrugged his shoulders. "They are nice, I guess," he said. "Miss Sophy once gave me a drink of water out of a glass."

When they reached the Auld house, Fred was highly pleased with their reception. The owners, Mr. and Mrs. Auld, were at the front door to meet them. Behind his mother, clinging to her skirts, was little Tommy.

"Welcome to Baltimore, Fred," Mr. Auld said. "And, Rich, thank you for bringing him."

Rich knuckled his forehead in the humble way of plantation Negroes. He would have left right away, but Mrs. Auld stopped him. "The cook will give you some food, Rich," she said. "You know where to go."

After Rich left for the kitchen, Mrs. Auld drew Tommy out from behind her. "Tommy, this is Freddy," she said, putting Tommy's chubby little hand into Fred's lean brown hand. "Freddy will help to take care of you and be kind to you. Won't you, Fred?"

Fred, holding Tommy's hand, was all but tongue-tied by this pleasing statement. "Yes, ma'am," he managed to say.

Mrs. Auld seemed satisfied. She smiled and said, "Now we'll show you where you are to sleep, so you'll begin to feel at home."

She led the way through the hallway and up carpeted stairs to a little room. "This will be your room here, Fred," she said. "Tommy's room is next door."

Fred, hesitating on the threshold, could

scarcely believe his eyes. Here was a bright, clean room with a window! There was a real bedstead and real covers! There was a chest of drawers and a stand with a bowl and pitcher.

Mrs. Auld gave Fred a little push. "You may use the water in the pitcher to wash your hands and face," she said. "Tommy and I will go to his room. Then you may come there."

At his new mistress' suggestion, Fred poured water into the bowl and washed his face and hands. Then he walked slowly around the room, touching everything. He sat briefly on the bed, which was soft like the sofa in Captain Anthony's parlor. He opened drawers and discovered special clothes intended for him.

"This must be the Promised Land!" he whispered, thinking of the words to the spiritual he'd first sung to Miss Lucretia. "I've sailed over, and now I'm viewing it!"

Fred was greatly pleased with the treatment

106

he received in the Auld home. Neither Hugh nor Sophia Auld had ever had a slave before, and both treated him like any other child. If Tommy got a treat, so did Fred. He was accepted, in fact, as a member of the family.

Naturally, in this atmosphere, Fred's attitude changed, too. Instead of speaking to these white folks only in as few words as possible, he really talked with them. And he dared to look at them as he spoke without fearing they would think he was impudent.

Hugh Auld was a shipbuilder. Shortly after Fred's arrival, he got some new contracts which required him to spend more and more time away from home. One day Fred overheard him ask his wife, "Do you think you can manage Fred alone, my dear?"

"Yes, I certainly can," she replied. "After all, he is only nine years old."

"Well," said Hugh, not sounding too sure,

"keep him busy. I've heard that idle slaves often become trouble-makers."

Fred held his breath for a few seconds, waiting for Mrs. Auld's reply. "He's only a child," she said.

Fred let out his breath again with a sigh of relief. Mrs. Auld really was different from anybody he had ever known before. She didn't think of him as a piece of property, even when reminded that he was a slave.

Mrs. Auld managed to keep Fred busy watching five-year-old Tommy. He held Tommy's hand when they walked to the playground. He took a tight grip on the child's clothing to keep him from falling into the duck pond. He played, really, the role of a responsible big brother.

As the months went by, Fred grew more and more accustomed to kind treatment instead of abuse. Mrs. Auld often smiled at him. When she held Tommy on her knee, she encouraged Fred to sit on a footstool close by. Often she read aloud to both boys from the Bible.

Fred had never heard anyone read before. He was fascinated by the book which told Mrs. Auld what sounds to make. One day, he

chanced to be alone in the room where the Bible was. Hesitantly he opened the book and stared at the rows of black print. How did they tell Mrs. Auld what sounds to make?

Mrs. Auld entered the room and saw Fred looking at the open book. "What are you doing, Fred?" she asked.

Fred, taken by surprise, started. "No harm, I hope," he said quickly.

Mrs. Auld smiled. "Perhaps I should have asked, 'What are you trying to do?'"

"To find out how you know what words to say," Fred answered. "I'd like to say them, too."

Mrs. Auld looked pleased. "You mean you'd like to learn how to read, Fred? How wonderful! We'll begin at once."

She kept her word, using the family Bible as Fred's textbook. First she pointed out a small "a" and a large "A" and said them aloud. Fred looked and repeated after her. Then she turned

110

a page and had him find both the small and large letters for himself. After he had proved that he knew them, she went on the "b's" and the "c's," "d's," and "e's" before she stopped the lesson for the day. "You're a very good pupil, Fred," she said with a smile.

Fred didn't know what she meant, but he could tell she was pleased with him. "Tomorrow we'll continue," she promised.

Learning a few letters at a time, Fred soon became master of the printed alphabet. Shortly he could read and spell words of three or four letters. "You'll soon be reading the Bible for yourself," Mrs. Auld said.

The next day Hugh Auld came home unexpectedly and found Mrs. Auld giving Fred his lesson. "Sophia what do you think you're doing?" he almost shouted.

"Teaching Fred to read," she replied simply. "He's a very apt pupil."

111

"Well, stop teaching him at once!" Mr. Auld commanded rather sharply. "It's unsafe to teach a slave to read."

"Why?" she asked, shocked. "How can it be unsafe for anybody to read God's word?"

"Well, it would be all right if he'd be content just to read God's word, but he wouldn't," Hugh Auld continued. "The first thing you know, he'll be reading anti-slavery literature. Then who knows what he'd do? We might not even be safe in his company. I tell you, Sophia, the only good slave is an ignorant slave!"

Fred heard Hugh Auld's words with a sinking heart, because he knew that they were bound to influence Mrs. Auld. As he thought about them later, however, he realized that they gave him a partial answer to the question of what made some people slaves and some people free. The secret was simply this—knowledge or the lack of it made the difference.

"Sometime, when I know enough, I'll know how to gain my freedom," Fred said to himself. "And when that day comes I'll really be free!"

By his actions today, without knowing it, Hugh Auld had done Fred a great service. He had set his feet on the long pathway that led from slavery to eventual freedom.

A Giant Step

AFTER HUGH AULD objected to his wife teaching Fred to read, she did an abrupt about-face. She not only made no further effort to teach Fred, but also tried to keep him away from all manner of reading matter.

The seeds of learning, however, had been planted in Fred's mind. He was determined to continue his education, although at the moment he did not know how he would manage it.

From time to time as Fred had run errands for Mrs. Auld, he had made the acquaintance of white boys running errands for their parents. Occasionally they had enjoyed a bit of sport together, as playing marbles, spinning tops, or broadjumping. Afterwards, they had sat on the curb to rest and had talked about things that concerned them. Bit by bit Fred had told them what it was like to be a slave.

Quite naturally, he told the boys his sad tale the next time he saw them. They found it hard to believe, because in Baltimore most slaves were well treated. "That treatment by Mr. Auld wasn't fair," one of the boys declared.

"It must be illegal!" said another.

"I wouldn't stand for it," said a third, "but I guess you'll have to."

All the boys sat thinking and talking for a few moments. Finally a fourth boy said, "I know what we can do, Fred. *We* can teach you."

That idea pleased everybody. The boys at once provided Fred with a dog-eared copy of Webster's spelling book. They brought him their papers from school and scraps of newspaper.

From then on, whenever Fred and his friends met on the street, they didn't waste time playing games. They played school, instead.

One day, about three years after Fred had come to Baltimore, something happened that threatened to prove far more upsetting to him than Hugh Auld's unfairness. Through the years he had come to believe that he belonged to Mr. Auld, but he was mistaken. He still belonged to his old master, Captain Anthony.

Fred discovered this fact to his sorrow in the summer of 1829, when Captain Anthony died. He was now part of the property that had to be divided between Captain Anthony's children, Andrew and Lucretia. He had to return to the plantation to be valued and reassigned.

The state of affairs greatly distressed Mrs. Auld and her son Tommy. She had come to think of Fred almost as a son, and Tommy had come to think of him as a brother. All three shed tears when they had to say good-by. Who knew whether they would ever meet again?

Fred still realized that he was a slave, but he had become used to being treated like a human being. Therefore, what happened to him when he returned to the plantation came as a shock. He was shut into a pen with dozens of other slaves, including men, women, and children of all ages and conditions of health.

Alongside this pen were other pens, some bigger, some smaller, which contained horses, sheep, cattle, and pigs. Both people and animals, Fred learned, had to be closely examined to determine their value. Their arms and legs were pinched, their teeth inspected, their eyes and ears tested for soundness. Each was then tagged to show what he was supposed to be worth.

At first, Fred felt very low in spirits. He knew that he wouldn't be considered of very high value. He was still only twelve years old, too young to work in the fields. And he wondered what use he could be to either the Thomas Aulds or to Andrew Anthony.

Soon he began to hear dreadful things about Master Andrew. Most of the other slaves had a horror of falling into his hands. He had a bad disposition and besides was often short of money. When this happened, he would sell anything he owned at public auction.

Fred was frightened. He felt that he just wouldn't want to live if he were awarded to Andrew. In his fright he fell on his knees in the mire of the slave pen. Then, remembering words from the Lord's Prayer, he cried, "Oh, Lord, please deliver me from evil! And oh, please, help me in this trouble."

Eventually, the prodding and pinching and tallying were over. To Fred's sobbing relief, he was allotted to Lucretia Auld. He was so over-come with gratitude that he bent down and kissed the hem of her skirt. She looked down at him, impressed by his deep feeling. Then she said gently, "Get up now."

Fred arose and stood, head bowed, in the attitude expected of plantation slaves. To his surprise, Miss Lucretia put a finger under his chin and lifted his face. She gazed at him and shook her head slightly and said, "My, how you have grown, Fred! You're not the puny little boy I used to know."

"No, ma'am," said Fred.

Lucretia sighed. "You're still too young to be of any use to Master Thomas on the farm," she said, "and I have no use for a boy as big as you around the house."

Her words sent a frightening chill through Fred's body. Would she decide to sell him at public auction, as he had feared Andrew Anthony would do? He wouldn't bring much money, but he knew he was worth something.

"Well," Miss Lucretia said, "you seem to be very good with children. Mrs. Hugh Auld has told me how much Tommy loves you."

Fred could not help smiling as his heart lifted with hope. "Yes'm," he said meekly.

"I have a little daughter named Amanda," said Miss Lucretia. "Of course, she needs a little girl slave to keep her company, but I suppose you could drive her pony cart."

Fred had never driven anything in his life, but he nodded eagerly. "Well, we'll see," said Miss Lucretia. "Right now come on home with me. You could do with a wash and a meal."

Home, for the Thomas Aulds, was now a farm a few miles away. An overseer, Mr. Tracy, worked the farm with slaves provided by Miss Lucretia. Thomas Auld owned no slaves of his own and did not know how to manage them. He kept a general store in a nearby town and spent most of his time there.

The farm slaves were grateful for this arrangement. "Master Thomas can be real mean," they said, "and we'd rather take our chances with Mr. Tracy. Miss Lucretia keeps an eye on him."

Less than a week after Fred went to live on the farm, Thomas Auld decided to send him back to Baltimore. "Evidently my brother thinks you're some good to him," he said, "so we might as well let him continue to feed and clothe you."

Fred was delighted at the news. He could scarcely wait until he would see Tommy and Miss Sophy again. All he could think of were the things he had liked about living in Baltimore. The things he had not liked seemed to be of no account now.

His reunion with the Baltimore Aulds was joyous. Miss Sophy hugged him and cried. Tommy capered about like an organ grinder's monkey. Even Master Hugh clapped his shoulder and said, "Welcome home."

For the rest of the summer, Fred felt completely happy. He resumed his care of Tommy and took him daily to the park to play. He did small chores about the yard, such as scrubbing the white steps, clipping the grass, and burning the trash.

When fall came, Tommy started to school, and Fred had a new task. For a while he had to escort Tommy back and forth morning and evening. Seeing Tommy go inside the halls of learning from which he himself was barred became very bitter punishment.

Fred began more and more to brood about the sadness of slavery. Sometimes he saw Mrs. Auld looking at him with a puzzled expression. He longed to tell her that she started much of his misery. If she had never started him reading, he wouldn't know what he was missing. Instead, he would be just as happy as the little dog she had recently acquired, and just as dumb.

He seldom had a chance now to talk with the other white boys as he had done before, but one time he managed to have an important conversation with them. Though they had no chance to teach him anything, they were able to tell him about a book called *The Columbian Orator*, which they read in school. "We have to learn pieces from it to say out loud," one boy told him one afternoon.

"It's great!" said another. "It includes speeches by Patrick Henry and William Pitt and all sorts of famous people."

"You really ought to get a copy," said a third boy. "It even includes parts about slaves and freeing them."

"You can buy one at Mr. Knight's shop on Thames Street," volunteered a fourth boy.

As soon as Fred could, he made his way to Thames Street. Mr. Knight saw him peering wistfully into the window and came out to talk to him. "What do you want, boy?" he asked, in such a kindly voice that Fred felt free to tell him what he wanted.

Fortunately, Mr. Knight kept no slaves and did not approve of anybody else keeping them. He did not believe in keeping slaves ignorant either. "Do fifty cents worth of work for me and you may have the book," he said.

In this manner Fred secured the book which the boys had recommended. Acquiring it took him another big step along the road to freedom.

Fred Gets Ideas

FRED READ the new book thoughtfully page by by page and found it very comforting. It introduced him to the very sorts of ideas that Hugh Auld had been afraid he would discover. It taught him that men were willing to die rather than be enslaved. It showed him that many believed "all men were created equal."

He felt strengthened by what he read. The book supported many of his own ideas. God-up-in-the-sky did not make white people to be masters and black people to be slaves.

The next time Fred saw his white friends he told them how he felt. "That book you told me to read!" he cried. "It says that God didn't make anyone to be a slave!"

"We told you that we didn't think it was right for us to be free and you not to be free," they reminded him.

"Yes, but I didn't know any grown folks felt that way!" replied Fred.

"Many grown folks do," the boys explained. "Some of the bravest of them, called abolition-ists, are starting to do something about it."

"Ab-o-lition-ists," Fred repeated slowly. He remembered that he had heard the word spoken by Hugh Auld and his guests. Not knowing what it meant, he hadn't paid any attention. From now on, he would listen more closely.

Fred snatched every chance to be useful to Hugh Auld when company was around. He moved about the room serving delicacies to the visitors or fanning them when they were over-heated. He was so constantly present that guests paid no more attention to him than they paid to what he served.

One evening, when guests were present, Fred heard the word "abolitionist" repeated and repeated with increasing anger and bitterness. "The abolitionists are out to ruin us slaveholders," one guest declared.

"Yes, they would just as soon burn our houses with us in them," said another.

"They don't seem to realize that most of us treat our slaves exactly as we treat our children," Hugh Auld said.

At that, quite unconsciously, Fred shook his head, causing him to jiggle the bottles on a tray. The sound drew Hugh Auld's attention. "Watch what you're doing, boy!" he said.

"Yes, sir," said Fred.

His answer was polite enough, but something in the tone of his voice or his posture disturbed Mr. Auld. "We won't need you any more tonight," he said. "Take the tray back to the kitchen and go to bed."

Fred had no choice but to obey. As he left the room, he heard Mr. Auld say, "Little pitchers have wide ears," and the company laughed.

The comment puzzled Fred. Pitchers didn't have ears. They had mouths, but not ears!

After that evening, Fred heard no more talk of abolition when he was near. This made him sure it was something he wasn't supposed to know about. His curiosity increased.

One day, Mr. Auld carelessly left a copy of the *Baltimore American* lying about. Fred, eager for anything new to read, found the paper and hid it behind the drapery.

The paper proved to be a gold mine of information about abolitionists. It talked of a movement to abolish slavery in the District of Columbia. It spoke of a law to prevent slave trade between the states. Most important of all, it helped

Fred to discover that there were states where no slavery existed.

This news almost took Fred's breath away, for it put new hope into his heart. If the abolitionists became strong enough, maybe they could abolish slavery in Maryland someday. "With God's help, they might!" he thought.

He remembered how he had prayed that night in the slave pen. God had heard his plea and granted it, keeping him from falling into Andrew Anthony's hands.

"I haven't a right to ask God for anything more," Fred decided. "But maybe if lots of folks pray for freedom, God will listen."

The question was, where could he find people to pray? He didn't want to ask the Aulds. They would want to know why he was suddenly getting religion. Fortunately, Hugh Auld again played into Fred's hands. He decided that Tommy was able to walk to and from school now and that Fred could spend his time helping out at the shipyard. He would do odd jobs that didn't require skill.

Fred now had a chance to talk to all sorts of people. Among them was an old colored man, known as Uncle Lawson, who was a great believer in prayer. He prayed as he walked through the streets, while he worked, and everywhere. When he spoke, his words were most often about "the better world to come."

After Fred had known Uncle Lawson for a short time, the old man invited him to come to a prayer meeting at the Bethel Church. At this meeting Fred found people he had been seeking, persons like himself with whom he could pray.

Fred managed to attend a number of prayer meetings before Mr. Auld found out about them. "I forbid you to go there again!" he said. "If you do, I'll have to whip you."

Whipping was something Mr. Auld had never

threatened before. Fred was not afraid because he suspected that Mr. Auld really would not raise a hand to punish him. From then on, however, Mr. Auld watched Fred's movements so carefully that he found it hard to get away.

One day at noon, when Fred was idling on the wharf, he saw two white men laboring to unload a scow. He offered to help them and afterwards they thanked him. "That was a very Christian thing to do," they said.

"I was glad to help," Fred said.

The men looked at him curiously. "Are you a slave or a bound boy?" they asked.

A bound boy, Fred knew, was a boy bound to serve a master for only a limited time, but he didn't know any Negro who was that lucky. "I'm a slave, bound for life," he said.

"That's too bad for a nice upstanding young fellow like you," said one of the men.

"Why don't you run away?" asked the other.

"Go north, to Pennsylvania, a free state, and you'll likely find people to help you."

The idea of running away to a free state had never occurred to Fred. It was a new idea, but it was something he might do someday. His heart leaped with excitement.

"Of course, you'd have to carry papers saying you had a right to be where you are," the first man warned. "You'd have to be careful about talking with people, too. Masters usually pay good money for the return of slaves."

Fred suddenly realized Mr. Auld wouldn't approve of his getting friendly with strange white men. Besides, how did he know he could trust the men and how could he be sure they wouldn't report what he said to Mr. Auld? He swallowed hard, hoping his voice wouldn't squeak when he replied, "I have a good master and mistress. Why should I run away?"

The men exchanged glances and shrugged.

"Suit yourself," one of them said.

"Yes, go on being a slave," said the other.

The men turned their backs on Fred. He hesitated a moment, then walked slowly away from them. He was sorry to hurt them, if they were being kind, but how was he to know?

Fred was glad to work at the now familiar shipyard. He liked the clean smell of sawdust and the sharp scent of the pine tar used to fill holes. He liked to hear the rhythm of saws and the steady pounding of nails.

One day he noticed that the carpenters marked each piece of cut timber with what seemed to be a letter. After watching them a while, he asked what the purpose was.

The carpenters seemed glad to explain. "On a piece ready for the starboard side, we write 's,' and for the larboard side we write 'l.' For larboard forward we write 'l.f.' and for larboard aft, 'l.a.' Get it?"

Fred nodded. So this was writing! All he had ever seen was printing. Now he wanted to learn to write. "I'll teach myself," he decided. "Any educated person has to know how."

At first, he was at a loss for writing materials. Then, out of his early childhood, he remembered his grandmother's calendar. She had used a sharp stick to make marks in the damp earth. He could do the same.

Eagerly, he copied "a's," "f's," "s's," and "l's" until he could write them easily. As soon as he had a chance, he showed his white friends what he could do.

"Good for you," they said. "Now you'll have to learn all the other letters."

Fred's face fell. The carpenters didn't use any other letters that he knew about.

"We'll teach you," his friends offered.

When Fred discovered how many letters there were, he realized it wouldn't be safe to practice writing them in the earth of the shipyard. He would have to find some other means of learning and practicing.

What he found were used copybooks which Tommy had used at school. He took these to his own room and hid them. Only at night, after everyone else was in bed, did he dare get them out and practice.

The first long piece he copied was Patrick Henry's famous speech before the Virginia Convention. Afterwards, he reread it proudly, lingering on the ending. Somehow those strong final words, "Give me Liberty, or give me Death!" expressed his feelings exactly.

A Stubborn Mule
Needs Gentling

Six Months after Fred returned to Baltimore, Miss Lucretia died. He felt very sad on hearing the news, because she always had been good to him. Also, he felt a bit uneasy because he now belonged to her husband, Thomas Auld. For two years, however, Mr. Auld had given no sign of wanting him. Indeed, Fred had almost forgotten that Mr. Auld might want him.

But one day, Mr. Auld did. He soon married Rowena Hamilton, the daughter of an aristocratic slave owner. They lived near St. Michaels, a fishing village, where they entertained many friends. Soon she heard how well Miss Lu-

138

cretia had liked Fred and was determined to have him in her own household. Finally, Thomas picked a quarrel with his brother and demanded the return of his property.

Fred dreaded the thought of leaving Baltimore, but this time not so much because of leaving the Aulds as for leaving others. Most of the time recently he had spent away from the Auld home. Master Hugh had hired him out to do odd jobs for other people and often he had stayed where he worked. In this way, for the first time in his life, he had come to make many friends. Now he would miss seeing them.

The fact that he had to go made him feel very bitter. Once on board the sloop that would take him to St. Michaels, he clenched his fists and pounded the railing in desperation. What a fool he had been not to have run away when he had a chance! Now he was in a trap from which escape would be very difficult.

Fred had never really known Thomas Auld as the husband of gentle Miss Lucretia. He soon learned to know him now, however, as the husband of the haughty Miss Rowena. As a pair, they were difficult to please.

The thing that bothered Fred most about the Thomas Aulds was their stinginess with food. The slaves were allowed even less per week than on Lloyd's plantation. Usually their ration was half a peck of corn meal per person per week, barely enough to keep them alive.

As a result of these conditions, all the slaves were forced to beg or steal food. Fred, the only male among the house slaves, looked wherever he could for things to eat. Fortunately, he soon found a prize source of food in the kitchen of Miss Rowena's father.

Fred made this discovery one day by accident when he forgot to shut the barn door. Master Thomas's horse disappeared, and it was up to

Fred to find the missing animal. Fortunately, he was able to follow the hoof prints of the horse, which led to the stable where the horse had formerly been housed. When he started to get the horse, Aunt Mary, the cook, called to him. "Let the horse stay for a spell. I'm baking some tarts. Come have some."

Fred ate like a starving boy, and Aunt Mary clucked over him like a mother hen. When he left, she gave him a basket of food, which he shared with the others. By careful planning, they made it last several days.

After that, Fred deliberately neglected to shut the barn door to let the horse run away. Then he went after the horse and Aunt Mary gave him some food. This kept on happening even though Thomas Auld whipped him severely for his carelessness.

Finally one day Thomas Auld realized Fred was deliberately letting the horse run away.

"My whipping you hasn't done a bit of good," he said. "You have to be broken of your bad conduct. I've decided to lend you to Edward Covey for a year. Then we'll see whether you are ready to toe the line or not!"

Fred had already heard of Edward Covey, who had the reputation throughout the neighborhood of being a first-rate hand at breaking the spirit of young Negroes. Any master who could not control a young slave sent him to Covey. In exchange for conquering the young offender, Covey got the free use of his services.

Fred went to Covey's on January 1, 1834. In spite of his dread of what lay ahead, he walked quickly. It was a bitter cold day, and his clothing was very thin. Before he reached the end of his journey, he was chilled through.

Thomas Auld had told Covey nothing about Fred except that he was "stubborn as a mule and needed gentling." Covey didn't bother to ask Fred what he was trained to do. He merely gave orders and expected them to be carried out promptly. The penalty for awkwardness or slowness was repeated stinging of the lash.

For the first time in his life, Fred worked as a field hand. Since he had never done field work before, he was rather awkward and slow about doing things. Besides, as soon as he learned to do one thing well, he was ordered to do something else. As a result, he often heard the snap of the whip and felt it on his back. For six months, scarcely a day went by without his being whipped at least once.

Finally there came a sweltering day in August. Fred and three other men were at work in the treading yard. This was the place where wheat was trodden out of the straw by horses.

The job was a four-part job, and each part depended on the other. The first man guided the horses. The second man gathered up the trodden

wheat, and the third man fed it into a fan that blew the husks from the grain. The fourth man then measured the grain.

Fred was given the job of gathering up the trodden wheat, the hardest, hottest job of all. He worked mechanically for hours, from sunup to mid-afternoon. At last he became so exhausted and dizzy that he fell to the ground. Then with his last bit of strength, he rolled to a spot where there was some shade.

As soon as Fred collapsed, the chain of work stopped. Only the horses' feet kept moving. Up at the house, Covey missed the whirr of the fan. He came racing to see what was wrong. "Fred is sick," he was told.

"Is he?" snorted Covey. Then he looked at Fred lying on the ground and cried, "Get up!"

Fred tried, but he couldn't stand up. By now Covey was furious. "I'll teach you what it means to be sick!" he yelled.

He took the iron bucket in which Fred had been carrying wheat and beat him savagely on the head. Only when Fred fainted completely away did he stop.

Fred lay where he was until dark. Then he took off for the woods instead of dragging himself up to the house. There Sandy, a Negro from a neighboring farm, found him.

Sandy listened to Fred's story with horror and said, "Come along with me. I'm on my way to visit my wife. She's a free woman and has a hut not far from here."

Sandy's wife bathed Fred's wounds and bandaged them. She gave him something to eat. Then Fred asked Sandy's advice. "Should I go back to Covey's or try to escape?"

"It's almost impossible to escape from here," Sandy said. "We live on a neck of land surrounded by water. The only road out passes St. Michaels, where everybody knows you."

146

"I know, but if I go back to Covey, he will kill me," Fred said.

"No, he won't, if you do what I say," Sandy told him. "I was born in Africa and learned this trick from the tribal medicine man. There is a certain root which, if worn, protects its wearer from harm. I'll get you one."

At first Fred objected. He was a Christian and believed his faith should be in God, not in heathen magic. "I'm a Christian, too," Sandy said, "but I carry a root with me. The Bible says, 'Unto the pure all things are pure.' So where's the harm in carrying one?"

Fred was surprised to hear Sandy quoting the Bible, but what he said made sense. "All right," Fred said, at last. "I'll take your advice and carry a root."

Sandy gave Fred the root. Then he said, "Go back to Covey's. Walk up bravely to the house as if nothing had happened."

Fred followed this advice, and Covey didn't lift a finger against him. Fred was flabbergasted. Could the root be magic after all? Then he laughed at himself. It was Sunday, the day Covey treated as a day of rest. That included rest from all activity, even whipping.

Before Fred had left Baltimore, Uncle Lawson had given him a Bible. He had not had much time to read it, but now he got it out to look up a quotation which he remembered. He found it in Paul's letter to the Colossians.

Slaves, obey in everything those who are your earthly masters. Whatever your task, work heartily, as serving the Lord and not men . . . for the wrong doer will be paid back for the wrong he has done.

The last words were the important ones. Then and there, Fred made up his mind. He would do exactly as Covey said, as well as he possibly could. Then, if Covey tried to beat him anyway, he'd defend himself.

148

"I'll show Covey that I'm a man just as he is," Fred vowed. "He has beaten me unjustly for the last time."

Fred meant what he said, and proved it. The next time Covey started to hit him, he resisted. When Covey kept on, he gave Covey blow for blow. His aim was not to injure Covey but to keep Covey from injuring him.

After a while, Covey gave up. In the six months remaining of Fred's year of service, he never tried to beat Fred again. Fred did not know quite whom to thank for his deliverance, but he suspected that he and Sandy both had been instruments of God's will.

Fred Turns Teacher

Fred Returned to Thomas Auld's on Christmas Day, 1834. He expected to resume the same chores he had done before he was sent to Covey's. His master, however, had other plans for him, and one week later sent him out on loan to another neighbor, William Freeland.

The boy who walked to Mr. Freeland's was a different boy from the one who had walked to Covey's the year before. He was larger and stronger, and he was determined never to submit to inhuman treatment again.

He soon discovered at Freeland's that he would not be treated harshly. Mr. Freeland was

150

a gentleman in every sense of the word. He acknowledged that his workers were people, not animals. He gave them plenty to eat and plenty of time for eating. He worked them hard during the day, but gave them full nights of rest. Moreover, he supplied them with modern tools.

If Fred had been a typical slave, he would have been contented at Freeland's. On the other hand, the good treatment made him long for something better. More and more often, he remembered his last months in Baltimore. There he had been able to talk with people who knew about things besides crops and cattle.

Fortunately, he found companionship in his two books, the Bible and the *Columbian Orator*. Now that he had time on his hands, he could read them again. He carried one or the other inside his shirt when he went to the fields. Then during his break for lunch he refreshed his mind by dipping into them.

Before long the other slaves became curious about Fred and his book They had never known a slave who could read. "Is it hard to learn how to read?" Henry Harris asked.

"Not if you put your mind to it," Fred said.

"Could we learn?" asked Henry's brother.

Instantly Fred's heart leaped at the idea of helping others. He would do for these slave boys what the Baltimore street boys had done for him. He would teach them to read!

"You can if you want to learn bad enough," Fred answered.

Good masters, like William Freeland, gave their slaves Sunday off to rest. Therefore, Fred decided that Sunday would be a good day for teaching the other boys. Of course, they'd have to gather someplace where their masters wouldn't find them. Rural slaveholders felt much like the slaveholders in Baltimore. The only good slaves were ignorant ones.

Fred's school proved very popular. News of it spread from farm to farm. Before long he had forty pupils, and he succeeded in teaching most of them how to read. The results were remarkable, because the boys were not free to give full attention to learning. They always were fearful of discovery and punishment.

Throughout the remainder of the year, Fred conducted his school without being discovered. At the end of the year he returned to Thomas Auld's for the Christmas holiday. He felt happy about his school, but he still was a slave, subject to his master's bidding.

The year 1836 started with Fred's condition unchanged. Mr. Freeland had asked for him again, and he was thankful not to have to walk into a new situation. Once more he returned to familiar surroundings and to friends.

During the previous year, Fred had used the Bible as his teaching book, but now he used the

Columbian Orator. Somehow as he went over the readings on human rights, which it contained, they aroused him more and more. The Declaration of Independence, in particular, fired him to discuss escaping and freedom with his friends, Henry and John Harris.

"Thomas Jefferson said that all men have the right to 'life, liberty, and the pursuit of happiness,'" Fred explained. "We have life but not liberty. And we cannot seek happiness because we're not free."

"Jefferson said these things, but did he mean them?" asked Henry.

"Yes, he freed his own slaves," said Fred, "so he meant what he said."

"Well," said Henry thoughtfully.

Shortly, Fred and the Harris boys were ready to act to secure freedom. They fully understood what they had to do. They would have to go "north," as far north as possible. They would have to get to a big city, where they might have a chance to get lost in the crowd.

It was actually only a short distance from eastern Maryland to the free states of Pennsylvania and New York, but Fred and his friends didn't know how close these states were because they had never seen a map. They were chiefly concerned about the dangers they would face along the way. There was the danger of hunger and thirst. There was the danger of traveling through strange country and the danger of being attacked by wild animals.

All these were hazards which anyone might face making such a trip on foot. For escaping slaves, however, there were extra hazards. These included slave hunters armed with guns and dogs that might tear a victim apart.

Fred and the Harris boys were aware of these dangers but were willing to face them. They took as their rallying cry Patrick Henry's

"Give me Liberty, or give me Death!" Another slave, Sandy, who had given Fred the "magic" root, begged to be included. Fred, remembering Sandy's kindness to him, reluctantly agreed.

The boys arranged a definite plan for their escape. They would take a large canoe on the shore of Chesapeake Bay and paddle to the head of the bay. There they would land, set the canoe adrift, and start northward on foot, using the North Star as their guide.

The boys chose the Saturday night before Easter Sunday as the time for their departure. Both Sunday and Monday were to be holidays, so they would not be missed for at least two days. As a further safeguard, Fred wrote out passes for the others, signing them with their masters' initials. These would serve as a protection if somebody stopped them at the outset. The passes read: "This is to certify that I, the undersigned, have given the bearer full liberty to go to Baltimore for a few days to spend the Easter holidays."

Everything seemed to be working smoothly until the morning they were to leave. Then suddenly at breakfast time, a group of white men armed with chains and whips appeared. "We are betrayed!" whispered Fred. "Swallow your passes!"

Soon it became obvious that the betrayer was Sandy, who was the only person not captured and bound. The other three, including Fred, were dragged fifteen miles to Easton. There they were put in jail, each in a separate cell.

The usual penalty for this sort of crime was sale to traders in the deep south states of Georgia, Alabama, Mississippi, and Louisiana. Slave life there was reportedly worse than death. The probability that this sort of life was in store for Fred and his friends made Fred feel miserable. He had got them into it.

Wonder of wonders, everything turned out much better than the boys anticipated. Thanks to Fred's quick thinking, the other boys had swallowed their passes, too, and there was no proof that they had planned to escape. Their masters, realizing that they were good workers, decided to keep them.

Fred's fate was in the hands of Thomas Auld, who considered his arrest as the last straw. "I can't be bothered with you any longer," he said, "and I won't have any peace as long as you stay in the neighborhood."

He paused, giving Fred a little time to worry about what he might say next. Then he added, "I've decided I was a little hasty in taking you away from my brother, so I'm going to send you back to Baltimore. Now that you're nineteen years old, it's high time for you to learn a trade."

Scenes in Baltimore

HUGH AULD found Fred a job as apprentice in William Gardiner's shipyard in Baltimore. Supposedly Fred was to spend his time learning how to caulk ships to make them watertight. On the day Fred arrived, however, Mr. Gardiner received a hurry-up order to build two vessels for the United States. In all the excitement, no one had time to teach Fred anything. "Just try to do whatever the carpenters ask you to do," Mr. Gardiner told him.

Fred soon found that he had an impossible task. There were seventy-five carpenters, and often several called to him at once, asking him

160

to do this or that, as "Fred, bring that roller here," "Fred, go bring me a crowbar," or "Fred, come and turn this grindstone."

Every time a carpenter gave Fred an order which he failed to carry out, the carpenter became furious. He proceeded to call Fred names and to swear at him. Finally, one carpenter struck him in a fit of anger.

Fred saw red. He felt that this kind of treatment was unjustified and he struck back. He continued to strike back whenever any carpenter hit him. By now he was strong and felt safe in resisting the attacks of any one man.

Finally one day four carpenters ganged up on him and came at him from all sides. All wore heavy boots, with which they kicked, and two of them had weapons, a brick and a hand spike. Fred was barefooted and empty-handed. He fought valiantly but finally was brutally beaten. All the while the fight was going on, the rest of the carpenters stood by and watched without lifting a finger to help.

As soon as Fred was able, he staggered home. Hugh Auld was appalled by his appearance and by his story. Sophia Auld cried. She fussed over him as she had when he had first come to Baltimore. She washed the blood from his face. She bound up his head. She covered his wounded eye with a fresh beef steak.

"You'll have to do something about this outrage!" she said to her husband.

"I intend to," said Mr. Auld.

He took Fred to a magistrate's office and asked the magistrate to issue a warrant for the immediate arrest of Fred's attackers. "Who witnessed this alleged attack?" asked the magistrate.

"A whole shipyard of people," said Mr. Auld.

"But not you?" asked the magistrate.

"Of course not," replied Mr. Auld. "I was at my own place of business."

"Well, unfortunately, I must have the oath of a white person who witnessed the attack," said the magistrate.

"But here's the boy! Look at him!"

The magistrate shrugged his shoulders. "That's no proof that he was attacked," he said.

"Well, this certainly is an unfortunate state of affairs!" Mr. Auld cried, but he realized that there was nothing more he could do. According to law, slaves were not people but mere property. They could not give testimony, any more than animals could.

Mr. Auld did not require Fred to return to Gardiner's shipyard. Instead, he took him to a place on Fell's Point where he himself worked as a foreman. By now he had lost his own shipping business and had to work for others.

In his new situation, Fred rapidly became an expert caulker. By the end of the year he was earning the highest possible wage for the trade in Baltimore, a dollar and a half a day. Even though he earned this money, he could not keep it. All the money that he earned had to be turned over to his master. This was one of the cruel and unfair facts of slave life.

As Fred continued to work, he became disturbed about his salary. He discovered that all the other caulkers, many of whom were Negroes, got to keep their wages. The difference was that these Negroes were freemen.

"We once were slaves, too," one of them confided to Fred. "Luckily for us, our former masters were kind persons who sympathized with us and gave us our manumission papers."

"Manumission papers are papers setting us free," another explained.

"I know what they are," Fred said.

Fred noticed that his companions exchanged surprised glances and realized that his reply had been ungracious. He hastened to smooth the troubled waters by saying, "I know what they are because I've read about them in the *Columbian Orator*."

"You've read the *Columbian Orator!*" said the man who had explained the meaning of manumission. "Say, you ought to come to our club meetings. We often have debates there."

Fred asked for details about the club. The men explained that it was called the "East Baltimore Mental Improvement Society." Its members included the young freemen of the Fell's Point area. Young women could belong, too.

"But I'm not a freeman," Fred sorrowfully reminded his new friends.

There was a brief silence. Fred's spirits fell and he feared that he had ruined his chances to meet with the others. "Oh, well," came the answer. "You can come as a guest. There are many of us, and each member is allowed to bring one guest to a meeting."

Fred was happy about the opportunity to meet with the East Baltimore Mental Improvement Society. He met with the group often and made many new friends. Constant companionship with freemen and free women made Fred more and more dissatisfied with his lot. Why should he be a slave, and they be free? He felt that he was as good as they were.

He discussed the question with his friends. They sympathized with him but warned him not to do anything foolish. One of them, a young woman named Anna, whom he particularly admired, pleaded with him. "For my sake, be careful. You can't afford to take chances."

"For you, I will be," he promised.

Fortunately Fred realized that he must not arouse Hugh Auld's suspicions. Surely Thomas Auld had told his brother about Fred's previous plan to escape, for which he had been jailed. Whatever move he made now to escape

had to be slow and easy. He must be certain that his plan would work.

As a first step, Fred decided to acquire some money of his own. He learned that other slaves hired themselves out, giving their masters a fixed sum at the end of each week. If a slave made more than enough money to pay his master, he kept the extra amount.

Fred tried to get permission from Hugh Auld to hire himself out. Finally, he convinced Mr. Auld that the arrangement would be beneficial to both of them. He would board and clothe himself and give Mr. Auld the prescribed amount every Saturday night. Formerly, Mr. Auld had been responsible for all of Fred's keep.

Fred congratulated himself on making the first step safely, and for months the system seemed to run smoothly. He worked long and hard and made enough money so that he could actually save some for himself. Then came a

Saturday night when he did not deliver his master's share of the money on time.

On that night Fred had decided to attend a religious revival meeting outside of town, which lasted longer than scheduled. By the time he returned to Baltimore, the night was already far advanced. Since he knew the Aulds were already in bed, he decided to wait until morning to deliver Mr. Auld's money.

This was a serious mistake on Fred's part. His master was furious and said, "How dare you go out of the city without my permission?"

"Sir," replied Fred, "I understood that my time was my own as long as I paid you your share of my earnings."

"You are bound to show yourself here every Saturday night," replied Mr. Auld. "Now you have cooked your own goose. You can no longer hire yourself out for pay."

Fred returned to live with the Aulds, but not

happily. He had lived as a freeman for months. Now he found it all the more difficult to endure being treated like a slave again.

All the rest of that summer, he sought ways and means of making a safe escape. He told a few of his friends what he planned to do, and they promised to help him.

The freeman who finally came to Fred's rescue was a sailor whom he had met on the docks. This sailor, knowing that a traveling Negro could be asked at any time for his "freedom papers," offered Fred his own seaman's papers. He himself could get others, he said, on the ground that he had lost the original ones.

On Monday, September 3, 1838, Fred said goodby to Baltimore and to the life of slavery he had hated and resented for so long.

Free at Last

WHEN FRED finally escaped, he looked like an honest seaman wearing an old red shirt, tarpaulin hat, and black cravat tied sailor-fashion. He could talk much like a sailor, thanks to the years he had spent in the shipyards and around the docks. He had nothing to fear, unless someone looked closely at the papers which he carried. Unfortunately, these papers described a person smaller and darker than he was. Therefore he had to dodge showing them, if he could.

Luck seemed to be with him from the start. The hack driver who gave him a lift to the station bought him a railroad ticket. When the conductor on the train came by some distance from Baltimore, he said, "I suppose you have your free papers with you."

At first Fred was taken by surprise and could think of nothing to say. He merely stared at the conductor for a few moments. Then, regaining his composure, he said, "Yes, sir, I have some papers with an American eagle on them. They will carry me around the world!"

He started to take the papers out of his pocket, but the conductor walked on without waiting to look at them. Now that he was past the point of greatest danger, he gave a sigh of relief, but he realized that he would still have to be careful until he left the state of Maryland and passed through the state of Delaware. Someone along the way still might recognize and betray him before he could get off the train at Wilmington, Delaware, and take a steamboat for Philadelphia, Pennsylvania.

When he reached Philadelphia safely, he felt light-headed with joy. He felt that the chain of bondage which he had carried all his life was broken. He still had to take a train to New York, but he really was no longer afraid. Pennsylvania was a free state and he would have nothing to fear from now on.

He reached New York safely, but suddenly his joy was diluted. By chance he met another fugitive slave, named Jake, whom he had known in Baltimore. "New York is full of Southerners who have come up here on trips," Jake said. "And there are many free Negroes here who act as spies. They hang out on the wharves and in the railroad stations, waiting to catch runaways like us. Don't trust anybody!"

"I plan to go to a colored boarding house here," Fred said. "Certainly I'll be safe in a place like that."

Jake shook his head. "Don't go to a colored

173

boarding house," he said. "It won't be safe. Try to find some other place to live."

With that warning, Jake went away, leaving Fred staring forlornly after him. "What can I do now?" Fred asked himself.

He still had a little money left, but he knew it wouldn't last long. At first he had planned to seek a job as a caulker on the waterfront or in a shipyard, but now he realized that this wouldn't be safe. He must try to find something different to do, because this was the very kind of work Mr. Auld would expect him to do.

For several days he wandered around like a lost soul, sleeping in doorways and eating only what he could buy from street vendors. At last he decided that in spite of Jake's warning he had to trust someone. Finally he explained his problem to a friendly sailor.

Again, luck was with him. The sailor took him to David Ruggles, who helped to manage

174

the underground railway, an undercover means of helping slaves escape to the North. He took Fred to his home and found him temporay work.

Fred poured out his life story to Mr. Ruggles. He even told him about Anna, the free woman he had met at the Mental Improvement Society, saying he hoped to marry her someday. He hoped that Anna could come up North, too.

"We'll get her up here so that you can marry her," said Mr. Ruggles. "Then we'll help the two of you to go on to New Bedford, Massachusetts, where most people are abolitionists. Besides, New Bedford is a whaling town. You'll be able to find your kind of work there."

Soon Anna came up from Baltimore and she and Fred were married. Then they took a steamboat from New York to Newport, Rhode Island, where they transferred to a stagecoach to complete their trip to New Bedford.

When they arrived at New Bedford, they

were met by another underground conductor, Nathan Johnson. A new last name was necessary, Johnson explained, because the name Fred Bailey would be too easy to trace.

"How does the name 'Douglass' sound to you?" Nathan Johnson asked. "Douglass is the name of a great character in a book that I'm reading, called *The Lady of the Lake*."

Fred felt that it would be a good omen to take on a literary name, and Anna readily consented. Accordingly, from that moment onward Frederick Bailey, the slave, ceased to exist. In his place Frederick Douglass, a free man, came into being. This adoption of a new name was a great step forward in Fred's career.

In New Bedford, the new "Frederick Douglass" felt really free. He was treated like any other hard-working citizen by most of the people. The exceptions, sadly enough, were the owners of the shipyards where he wanted to

work as a caulker. "The men will quit if I hire a Negro," one such owner told him.

After young Douglass found that he could not work in the shipyards, he turned to other kinds of jobs. He worked in a whale-oil refinery, carrying barrels of oil. He worked in a brass foundry, operating bellows and swinging a crane. Everything he did required great strength but little brain power. In the evening, he was too tired to read before falling asleep.

"I wish there was a Mental Improvement Society here," he said to Anna. "I need something to shake up my brains!"

"Yes," Anna replied, but she didn't really miss the Society as much as he because she had joined to meet people. She never had come to enjoy reading as much as he enjoyed it.

Shortly after this conversation, a young man gave Douglass a copy of the *Liberator*, an abolitionist paper edited by William Lloyd

Garrison. As Douglass read this paper he was fired with an excitement such as he never known before. Sight unseen, he loved its editor and all the wonderful people who wrote for it.

The *Liberator* took second place only to the Bible in Douglass' heart. It detested slavery and slaveholders. It demanded nothing less than the complete emancipation of Negroes everywhere in the United States.

Douglass waited for announcements of all anti-slavery meetings held in New Bedford. He attended the meetings, listened to the great speeches, and applauded their words with enthusiasm. But for the first three years of his free life, he never spoke up for the cause.

In the summer of 1841, when he was twenty-four years of age, a grand anti-slavery convention was called on Nantucket Island, with William Lloyd Garrison as the chief speaker. Douglass had never taken a holiday since he arrived in Massachusetts, but he decided to attend the meeting to see his hero in person.

When Douglass arrived at Nantucket Island, a man from New Bedford, who knew his story, asked him to tell the audience about his experiences as a slave. Douglass trembled at the thought of speaking to a large crowd, but he allowed the man to lead him to the stage.

At first his voice cracked as he spoke, but it soon smoothed out as he warmed to telling the story of his life. He soon realized that he had the sympathy of his audience, for he heard shocked exclamations and even sobs. When he sat down, he was dripping wet with perspiration from his ordeal, but he was happier than he had ever been before.

At the close of the meeting, Douglass was asked to become an agent for the Massachusetts Anti-Slavery Society. His job would be simply to go about the state telling his life story. It was

180

felt that no one could plead the case against slavery as eloquently as someone who had actually lived and suffered under it.

Douglass could not refuse, for his heart and mind were both dedicated to the ideal of freeing the slaves. He was careful, however, as he went about the state, to use fictitious names and places. He hoped that these would mask his identity should the Aulds hear about the fugitive slave who had become a public speaker.

Champion of
Human Rights

LARGE CROWDS assembled to hear Douglass
when his appearances were advertised. People
traveled miles and miles to see him and to hear
him speak. Fugitive slaves were still rare then,
and a slave lecturer was a curiosity.

During the first few months, Douglass spoke
chiefly of his own experiences, and every new
audience was shocked. In this way he revealed
what the true conditions of slavery were like.

Garrison was delighted. "You really tug at
their heartstrings," he said. "You're just what
this movement needs!"

Gradually Douglass began to tire of telling

the same story over and over. He felt much like a machine, with only one tune to play. Besides, he had been doing extensive reading and thinking about the wrongs of slavery. Now he was eager to denounce the institution in moral and legal language.

Finally Douglass began to talk directly about the evils of slavery, but each time his fellow lecturers objected. "Just give the facts as you lived them, and let us take care of the philosophy," they said.

For a while, Douglass would try to follow these directions. Then his desire to moralize would get the better of him again. In words that were not only eloquent but Biblical, he called down God's wrath upon the southern tryants.

"People won't believe you were ever a slave, if you talk like an Old Testament prophet," said one of the general agents of the Society.

This agent was right. People began to doubt

Douglass was what he claimed to be. They came to believe that he had never been south of the Mason-Dixon line. "He doesn't tell us about his master or how he got away," they said. "Besides, he seems to be educated, and everybody knows slaves are ignorant."

Douglass wanted very badly to provide full information, but he realized that this would be dangerous. He was no longer guilty of just running away from slavery. He was also guilty of providing living proof of how brutally slaves were treated. Part of his lecture technique included removing his shirt, so the audience could see some of the great scars that had been left from whippings years before.

After a time, Garrison suggested that Fred write down the leading facts about his experience in slavery, including persons, places, and dates. Douglass complied and proceeded to write his *Narrative of the Life of Frederick*

Douglass, an American Slave. Then he deposited the manuscript in the files of the Anti-Slavery Society, praying that no one would stoop so low as to use it to destroy him.

The year 1843 was one of all-out anti-slavery activity in the northeastern states. One hundred conventions were held in a territory which included not only New England but also New York, Pennsylvania, Ohio, and Indiana. Douglass was one of the leading speakers chosen to assist in these meetings.

In most cities and towns, the delegates attracted wide attention and were received cordially. In only a few places were they treated roughly, where the audience shouted angrily at them or tried to injure them. At the end of the year, when the Society agents took stock of their accomplishments, they felt that, on the whole, the cause of emancipation had been advanced greatly.

"Now we need something to spark our campaign here at home," Garrison announced. "Let's think of what we can do."

Everybody thought, and soon Douglass spoke up. "Publish my *Narrative*," he suggested.

At first Garrison objected, but he admitted that publishing the manuscript might be "just the ticket." The chief problem was that it m' 'ht put Douglass's life in jeopardy. Then somebody came up with a solution to the problem. "Publish the manuscript and send Douglass to England for a year. He can blow the horn for abolition and enlist the British on our side."

Douglass went to the British Isles and was received with great enthusiasm. He was entertained by literary celebrities, politicians, philosophers, and religious leaders. He was invited to speak from many platforms about the evils of the slave system. He also listened sympathetically as people talked about some of the great British problems of the day, including the need to repeal the corn laws and the union between England and Ireland.

Douglass was very happy in England. He wrote Garrison, "I live a new life here. The spirit of freedom seems to animate all with whom I come in contact, and there is entire absence of everything that looks like prejudice against me on account of the color of my skin."

A few of Douglass' acquaintances in England conceived of a plan to ransom him from slavery. They learned that Thomas Auld would take one hundred and fifty pounds sterling for him and in return would send papers of manumission. They set to work soliciting funds from Douglass' many friends. Finally in the spring of 1847, they were able to hand Douglass the all-important document.

"What will you do in America now that you are a free man?" they asked him.

"I would like to establish a newspaper," Douglass said. "Presently there is no newspaper published regularly by and for the colored people of my country. I think there should be."

Once more Douglass' many friends dipped into their pocketbooks. This time they raised two thousand five hundred dollars to help him follow up his desires. Now he would be able to start a newspaper of his own.

Garrison was violently opposed to Douglass' plan and warned that it was sure to fail. Douglass insisted he wanted to give it a try, anyway, but that he would do it in territory where people did not read the *Liberator*. Accordingly, he moved his family, Anna and four children, to Rochester, New York. There among complete strangers he launched his new anti-slavery paper, the *North Star*.

The new venture succeeded but never brought Douglass great financial return. He managed to keep it going during all the years of national crisis from the autumn of 1847 until the outbreak of the War between the States. Then in 1863 emancipation became a fact.

Douglass did much more during those years than publish a newspaper. Since he lived near Lake Ontario, across from Canada, he became a conductor and used his home as a final station on the underground railway. In this manner he helped hundreds of fugitive slaves escape northward to freedom.

His friends and acquaintances included many literary figures and all the great abolitionists of the day. He even knew John Brown, who led the insurrection at Harper's Ferry that helped to hasten the War between the States.

During the war, Douglass met with President Lincoln to protest the unequal treatment which Negroes received while serving in the Union army. Lincoln promised to order that "justice

be done to the black race" and gave instructions to this effect to the Secretary of War. The results were disappointing, but Douglass had done what he could.

After the war, emancipation was no longer an issue. Now Douglass worked for passage of the fourteenth and fifteenth amendments, wh'ch guaranteed civil and voting rights to Negroes. He took an interest in politics and became an impressive figure at national conventions. Later he campaigned with Lucretia Mott and other suffragettes to win voting rights for women.

In order to be at the hub of things, Douglass moved to Washington, D.C., where he became adviser to several Presidents. President Ulysses S. Grant selected him one of five commissioners to consider annexing Santo Domingo to our country. President Rutherford B. Hayes appointed him Marshal of the District of Columbia, and President James A. Garfield appointed him

Recorder of Deeds. President Benjamin Harrison appointed him Consul-General to Haiti, the first Negro ever chosen to represent our country abroad.

In 1893, Douglass served as Haitian Commissioner at the World's Columbian Exposition in Chicago. He gave the formal dedication speech at the opening of the fair in January and helped to celebrate "Colored American Day" in August. At this celebration, which commemorated the progress made by American Negroes, he delivered the principal address.

This speech was his last prominent public appearance, but he continued to support the women's rights movement. He died February 20, 1895, a champion of human rights to the end.

Today the world honors Frederick Douglass, not just as a champion of human rights for Negroes, but as a champion of human rights for all.

More About This Book

WHEN FREDERICK DOUGLASS LIVED

1817   FREDERICK BAILEY WAS BORN IN SLAVERY NEAR TUCKAHOE, MARYLAND.

There were nineteen states in the Union.

James Monroe was President.

The population of the country was about 8,920,000.

1817–
1838   FRED LIVED AND WORKED ON A MARYLAND PLANTATION AND IN THE CITY OF BALTIMORE.

The Missouri Compromise was passed, limiting the extension of slavery, 1820.

The Monroe Doctrine was issued, 1823.

The Erie Canal was completed, 1825.

Peter Cooper built the first steam locomotive in the United States, 1830.

The first issue of the abolitionist periodical, the *Liberator*, was published, 1831.

Samuel Morse invented the telegraph, 1835.

American settlers reached Oregon, 1836.

1838– 1847	DOUGLASS FLED TO MASSACHUSETTS AND BE- CAME AN ACTIVE ABOLITIONIST.

Charles Goodyear perfected the method of vulcanizing rubber, 1839.

The United States acquired the Oregon Territory south of forty-ninth parallel, 1846.

The Mexican War was fought, 1846–1848.

1847– 1863	DOUGLASS PUBLISHED AN ABOLITIONIST NEWS- PAPER IN ROCHESTER, NEW YORK

Gold was discovered in California, 1848.

Harriet Beecher Stowe's *Uncle Tom's Cabin* was published, 1852.

The War between the States was fought, 1861–1865.

President Abraham Lincoln issued the Emancipation Proclamation, 1863.

1863– 1895	DOUGLASS HELD SEVERAL GOVERNMENT POSI- TIONS AND FOUGHT FOR HUMAN RIGHTS.

The Thirteenth Amendment to the Constitution, forbidding slavery, was ratified, 1865.

Thomas Edison invented the electric light bulb, 1879, and the moving picture, 1889.

Henry Ford built his first gas engine, 1893.

FREDERICK DOUGLASS DIED IN WASHINGTON, D.C. FEBRUARY 20.

There were forty-four states in the Union.

Grover Cleveland was President.

The population of the country was about 69,470,000.

DO YOU REMEMBER?

1. How did Fred happen to live with Aunt Betsey when he was a small boy?

2. Why did Aunt Betsey suddenly take Fred to a new place to live?

3. What did Fred see as Sarah and Perry showed him around his new surroundings?

4. How did a visit from his mother cause Fred to realize that he was somebody's child?

5. How was Fred shocked one day when he went to visit Old Barney at the stables?

6. How did Fred win the respect of his master's daughter, Lucretia Auld?

7. Why was Fred sent to Baltimore to become a house servant for Mr. and Mrs. Hugh Auld?

8. How did Fred get an opportunity to learn to read while he worked for the Aulds?

9. Why was Fred sent back to the plantation for a short period of time?

10. How did Fred learn about the abolitionist movement while he worked for the Aulds?

11. What happened when Fred and others tried to escape while working for William Freeland?

12. How did Fred get an opportunity to associate with freemen while he worked in Baltimore?

13. Why did Fred take a new name after he reached New Bedford, Massachusetts?

14. What were Frederick Douglass' leading accomplishments after he found freedom?

IT'S FUN TO LOOK UP THESE THINGS

1. What large bay extending north and south almost cuts Maryland in two?

2. What kinds of crops were grown on the low, flat plantations of eastern Maryland?

3. What kinds of work did slaves have to do on these plantations?

4. Why were shipping and shipbuilding important kinds of work in Baltimore?

5. How did the Underground Railroad operate to help slaves escape northward to freedom?

6. How did many slaves obtain freedom and continue to live in slave territory?

INTERESTING THINGS YOU CAN DO

1. Draw a map of Maryland including Baltimore, to show where Frederick Douglass lived.

2. Collect pictures of early homes in Baltimore and eastern Maryland for an exhibit.

3. Find out how ships were built in the days when Douglass was a boy.

4. Locate the Mason-Dixon Line and explain its relation to slavery.

5. Give a report on the rise and growth of the abolitionist movement in the North.

6. Name prominent Negroes besides Frederick Douglass who escaped from slavery.

7. Explain how Negroes helped the North win the War between the States.

OTHER BOOKS YOU MAY ENJOY READING

Flight to Freedom: The Story of the Underground Railroad, Henrietta Buckmaster. Crowell.

Frederick Douglass: Slave-Fighter-Freeman, Arna Bontemps. Knopf.

Harriet Tubman: Freedom Girl, Gertrude Hecker Winders. Trade and School Editions, Bobbs-Merrill.

Story of the Negro, Arna Bontemps. Knopf.

There Once Was a Slave: The Heroic Story of Frederick Douglass, Shirley Graham. Messner.

INTERESTING WORDS IN THIS BOOK

abolitionist (ăb′ō lĭsh′ŭn ĭst) : person who believes in doing away with slavery

abrupt (ă brŭpt′) : sudden, quick

aft (ăft) : toward the stern of a ship

anticipated (ăn tĭs′ĭ pāt′ĕd) : foreseen

apprentice (ă prĕn′tĭs) : young person bound by a legal agreement to work for another person in order to learn a trade

brandishing (brăn′dĭsh ĭng) : waving angrily or menacingly

198

brood (brōōd) : ponder, worry

callousness (kăl'ŭs nĕs) : lack of feeling

clairvoyant (klâr voi'ănt) : person who pretends to be aware of things others cannot see

cooper (kōōp'ẽr) : person who makes or repairs barrels

corn laws (kôrn lôz) : English laws controlling the export and import of foreign grains

crane (krān) : swinging arm for supporting kettles over a fire in a fireplace

diluted (dĭ lūt'ĕd) : weakened, diminished

dinghy (dĭng' gĭ) : small rowboat carried aboard a larger boat

disposition (dĭs'pō zĭsh'ūn) : temper

esteem (ĕs tēm') : regard, appreciation

fictitious (fĭk tĭsh'ŭs) : not real

flabbergasted (flăb' ẽr găst ĕd) : amazed, astonished

impudent (ĭm'pū dēnt) : abusive, rude

jeopardy (jĕp'ẽr dĭ) : danger

jib (jĭb) : small triangular sail extending from the foremast to the bow of a sailing vessel

larboard (lär'bōrd) : left side of a ship

larder (lär′dẽr) : room where food is stored in a home, pantry

magistrate (măj′ĭs trāt) : public officer with power to enforce laws, justice of the peace

plaited (plāt′ĕd) : braided

posture (pŏs′tŭr) : position of the body while standing, walking, or sitting

poultice (pōl′tĭs) : medicinal mixture on a cloth applied to the body to relieve pain

rankled (răng′k′ld) : irritated mentally or emotionally, upset

sloop (slōōp) : sailboat with one mast, a mainsail, and a jib

spit (spĭt) : pointed iron rod used to hold meat over a fire

starboard (stär′bōrd) : right side of a ship

tarpaulin (tär pô′lĭn) : waterproofed canvas which may be spread out to provide protection

testimony (tĕs′tĭ mō′nĭ) : statement provided by a person to help determine the truth

wheelwright (hwēl′rīt) : person who makes or repairs wheels or wheeled vehicles

Childhood

OF FAMOUS AMERICANS

CHILDHOOD OF FAMOUS AMERICANS